H.O.W?

How to Obtain Wealth in 30 days!

FINANCIAL SOLUTIONS TO FREEDOM

Anthony,
Thank you for your support.

Melvin D. Peterson
International Consultant and Educator

www. melvintalks. com

H.O.W? *How to Obtain Wealth in 30 days!*
IS A PETERSON PUBLISHING BOOK

Peterson Publishing Edition

Published by Peterson Publishing, Inc a division of Capital First Investments, LLC

Copyright © 2009 by Melvin Peterson
All rights reserved

Peterson Business Books
Peterson Books

Peterson Publishing
PO Box 167
Stone Mountain, GA 30086-0167

Peterson Publishing logo is a trademark of Peterson Publishing, Inc

Printed in the United States of America

First Printing September 2010

LCCN: 2010912466
ISBN: 978-0-578-06599-1

Overview

This book is for people who need alternative ideas to start generating income now. There is an old saying that goes "Good things come in small packages!" This miniature book will reveal many strategies that you can start implementing in your life now to generate unlimited income. Congratulations for investing in your financial future and you will find that your return on your investment will be more than what you have paid for the price of this book. Knowledge is not power, but applied knowledge will give you the power. Start applying the knowledge in this book and you will see that you will get paid a hundred times over from your initial investment.

Some of these strategies may be a little complex and may require additional due diligence. The contents in this book are ideas and strategies for obtaining alternative income and recommended that you consult with your financial advisor and/or legal professional to see if these strategies will work for you. This book is just a guide that will help give you additional ideas to generate income with little or no money out of your pocket. This book is only a guide and is not responsible for the capital gains or loss that you may incur from applying these principles. Always consult with professional and /or legal advisors to see if these strategies will work for you.

Money is an idea and the rich always find ways to create money by using their ideas. The rich understands the power of leverage and ROI (Return on Investment). While many people are scrambling to make ends meet, the rich are looking for multiple streams of income and ways to protect that income. The rich don't work for money; they have their money work for them even when they are asleep. The rich are producers the poor and middle-class are usually consumers. This is not a "get rich quick" book and will require additional research and due diligence on each strategy. This book is a guide that will open your mind to think outside of the box and allow you to start generating money within 30 days.

This book is a page-turner and you will find that getting unlimited income is just a page away. Practice one or all of these strategies and understand the risks and rewards when you get into a deal. Always remember the greater the risk the greater the reward. Use this self-help book and do not let it become a shelf-help book. Again, congratulations on making your first step towards learning how to start generating income in 30 days. Nothing comes to a sleeper but a dream; wake up and make your dreams come true by investing in your financial future today!

Melvin Peterson
Author, Consultant, and Educator

Table of Contents

1. How to Awaken the Millionaire Mindset?
2. I can't believe it's not MONEY!
3. Who stole your money?
4. How did I get a "mort" - "gage"?
5. How to "produce" wealth in Real Estate?
6. How to " produce" Intellectual Income?
7. How to "produce" income online?
8. How to "produce" income by Trading?
9. How to "produce" income in Network Marketing?
10. How can I transform into a cash flow producer?

CHAPTER 1

How to awaken the millionaire mindset?
Disturb the sleeping giant inside of you...

This book is designed to give you immediate alternatives to start generating income now. These strategies could open your mind of the possibilities in generating money. Many authors will identify the problem, but you are on your own to find a solution. This book is designed to give you specific solutions to help cure the cancer in your wallet. You have the option to use some or all of the recommendations to start generating cash. Many of these strategies can be used now to help you generate income with little or no overhead. True investors understand that it does not take money to make money. All you need is your ideas and the willingness to transform your ideas into money.

Everyone has the potential to be extremely wealthy. Create wealth in your mind and transfer it to your life. There are two creations. The first creation is in your mind, and the second creation is in reality. Regardless the direction of the economy, you have the potential to increase your financial prosperity by simply adjusting your mind towards financial freedom. The rich, middle-class, and the poor person share the same 24 hours in a day, but it seems that the financial statements from each of these categories are extremely different. Therefore, it is important to consider that what you do in your 24-hour day will determine the direction of your financial status. For instance, the rich do not care if we are in a recession, depression, or in a booming economy; the rich will get richer and the poor will get poorer regardless the direction of our economy.

The rich get richer because they know the value of wealth and understands that time is money. The rich invest their time and money instead of wasting time and money on consumer goods. Meanwhile, wealthy people invest while the poor and middle class consume. If you just break down the word consume, you will see how the middle class and the poor will self-destruct. This is the major difference from the rich and the poor. The root of the problem lies in our current educational system. The fundamental flaws of our economic system have their roots in ideas first popularized by Thomas Malthus, an English economist, in the early 1800s. If we stopped teaching Malthusian economics in our schools, we could change our national vision of the future. Instead of educating people from the point of view of scarcity, we should be educating them to look for abundance in exploring technology and productivity. It is crucial at this time to educate our children to look at the world as a place of great abundance. The people who look at how much they can give are the ones who will profit.

When we focus on sound economic principles and use them in our daily lives, we deliver more economic prosperity and you will see money pouring right in your pockets. You will see that life gets hard if you start saying to yourself, "What's in it for me?" True wealth comes by giving personal attention to how we can each make life easier for one another. It is a simple philosophy. If you give, you shall receive.

In our current educational system, we are doomed to widen the gap between the rich and the poor. In particular, the people most affected are the middle-class Americans. The reason for this is that the middle class will eventually cease to exist leaving only two categories for people to fall. Consider our educational system in the United States; we do not have a curriculum that will increase financial intelligence for students. The educational system does not teach you how to reach true financial freedom, they are conditioning our children to play it safe and do not make mistakes.

The educational system focuses time and energy in developing students to compete in a society that only values learning through memorization. Instead, students are not encouraged to foster entrepreneurial skills and creativity. In turn, they train to become employees rather than employers, followers rather than leaders. By studying to memorize certain facts and then forgetting about them once you pass your test is not developing your mind towards financial freedom. This process not only cripples your mind towards wasting countless hours and energy in memorizing pointless facts, but also keeps your financial genius asleep. Why should you memorize information that you find in books?

Many people believe that a problem solving stems from a single answer, without looking at the whole system. As long as we continue ignorantly to choose one "easy answer" at a time in an effort to cure our various social and economic problems, our society will continue to suffer. Successful systems produce successful results. Our educational system is not one of these Successful Systems. The educational system rarely supports and builds upon our natural learning abilities. Change begins with understanding the three kinds of learning and they are:

> 1. **Mental learning:** memorized facts, consisting of storing certain chosen data in our brains, much as we would file data in a computer.

2. Physical learning: a hands-on experience, involving all the senses, engaging most of the nervous system.

3. Emotional and subconscious learning: involving the student through feelings of joy, fear, sorrow, love, compassion, and exultation.

For true learning to occur, all three kinds of learning have to implement. Our educational system teaches that being right is more important than learning what you do not know. It rewards right answers and penalizes us for making mistakes. For example, I asked a student one day how he is doing in school. He responded, "I am doing great! I am on the honor roll and I get A's and B's!" He expressed enthusiastically. I asked him a follow up question, "When did you take your last test?" "I took one last week in Math and I got a 90% on the test so I got an A!" the student expressed. I then asked him, "Do you remember the questions that you got wrong?" "No!" the student responded, "I don't care because I passed the test and I got an A on my test" I thanked the child and he went on with his day.

It is important to look at the wrong answers. It is from the correction from our mistakes is the way we learn the best. Mistakes are much more important than the right answers. Today I see people that work for corporations or I should say "corpse-orations". Many people are walking zombies and acting snobby to people because they excelled academically and they think that they are better than others are.

Teaching only by memorization leaves people walking in one of two roads, both of the roads leads to self-destructions and dead ends. If they were good at memorization and did well on tests, they left school believing they were educated and smart, even though the only thing their good grades really measured was their ability to memorize. People with these kinds of beliefs never progress very far in life. Fearful of making a mistake, they constantly seek out environments where there is limited to no risk. Often they hold the same job for their entire lifetimes, all the while suffering unfulfilled dreams, insufficient salaries, and boredom. They become nerds in school and nerds in life, which stands for Never Ever Realizing Dreams. They know that something magical should happen in their lives, yet many of these nerds never get to experience it firsthand, because the implanted seed of mistakes over-rides their destiny to become financially free.

The second road is the one taken by people who do not memorize very well and society categorize these people as "not-so-smart". The school diminished their self-esteem early on in life. They believed in the labels that society placed on them. They think that they are stupid and they go through life accepting that they will not go far. These people hate making mistakes because each mistake only reinforces their belief that they are stupid. Many give up because they are unaware that the inability to memorize has no bearing on their potential for success. Some of the people on this road feel grateful just to have a job of any kind, even if they are just as unhappy as their "smart" counterparts are.

This is the cycle for many people in the world. They go to school, make good grades by memorization, and work for money for the rest of their lives and expect the company to take care of them. This thought process would keep your millionaire mindset asleep. This is the reason that this is the first chapter of the book and the most important chapter to grasp. Once you recognize that the educational system conditions people to be dependent on a system aka a "JOB", you will see that just having a "JOB" will cripple your millionaire mindset and the chance for you to be financially free will be obsolete.

So what is the solution?

One big piece of the answer is that we want to make more money without doing anything differently. We want to get richer without having to acquire any more knowledge. To receive more, we must give more, and to produce more, we need new information. This lack of information has brought down civilization after civilization throughout history.

Of all the methods of learning that are available to us, memorization is the most monotonous, the least challenging, and the most boring. The educational system emphasizes this type of learning instead of fixing the problem. We point fingers and it becomes a stalemate. It is like asking a fish to clean the water in the ocean. The situation has them so immersed that they cannot see that it is part of a larger system. Most of the people that we turn to for solutions are unable to see the larger picture. Meanwhile, we blame our educational failures on inadequate teachers, low pay, or class size, because this appears to be the problem. Most of us have a hard time dealing with what we cannot see.

The answer might be right there in front of us but we cannot see it. We will truly fix the education system if we incorporate the natural way we learn by implementing The Four Stages of Learning instead of dealing with the whole system. People learn at a different pace and at different times. You can divide the process into four stages: I will use a simple illustration of how a baby learns how to walk. This

illustration is a model of any type of true learning.
The Four Stages of Learning

> **1. Unconscious Incompetence:** The baby is excited about learning how to walk, but having never done it before the baby is unaware of what they have to learn.

> **2. Conscious Incompetence:** The baby stands up and starts to wobble but eventually put one foot in front of the other. The baby eyes are wide open and he really gets excited but quickly falls, making the baby aware that there are things that he does not know.

> **3. Conscious Competence:** Through trial and error, the baby corrects the mistakes. The baby observed, usually on an unconscious level, what he have been doing that causes him to fall and by trying different movements the baby finally become a competent walker.

> **4. Unconscious Competence:** The baby no longer thinks about what he is doing. The baby hold the knowledge he needs within him, and he automatically draw upon that knowledge as he walk.

Consciously or unconsciously, you are probably aware of this process of learning. Regardless of what a person wants to learn, the Four Stages of Learning makes it possible. Implementing this in our educational system will be a good place to start. This type of learning is naturally fun for us. The educational system puts an end to our fun. They substituted the fun and started boring us with the mental aspect, and forgot about teaching the physical and emotional part of the learning process.

Memorizing facts will be the cool thing to do if you are on the Jeopardy game show because knowing certain facts will get you paid. However, the average person does not have the opportunity to use the factual data that they have memorized from our educational system to appear on the show or in real life. It is unbelievable that I do not use much information past the 5th grade. The rich do not memorize a bunch of data to increase their wealth; they know where to find the information needed to make a sound financial decision towards building endless wealth. For example, Bill Gates dropped out of school in the pursuit of something greater than what an institutionalized educational system provides. He created a proven system and built a billion dollar empire from somebody else's idea. Mr. Gates built this empire from someone who was academically intelligent but did not understand systems. The rich surround themselves with a team of people to gain wealth, while others surround themselves with broke friends and take their advice. The banks never ask me how I did in school or if I made the honor roll on my report card. My banker never asked to see my report card. The only report card they want to see is my financial statements and my credit report.

The banks do not care if I memorized all of the formulas in my Physics class and the contents of the periodic table. They never asked for the location of the heart of a dissected frog that I performed in middle school. They never asked me if I knew the mass of the earth and the distance it is from the sun. Your financial statements and credit report is a major deciding factor for getting financing, and this should take priority.

I am not here to bash the educational system and give you a laundry list of all of the mishaps of the education system. I want to awaken the financial genius sleeping inside of you. Scholastic education is the fundamental requirements to develop financial intelligence. Knowing basic reading, writing, and arithmetic is critical to establish basic comprehension of certain facts. Scholastic skills are very important but it has its limitations. Some of the information that you learned in school might be useless after graduation.

Financial Intelligence is often obtained outside of school and considered an extracurricular activity because the educational system does not classify this topic as one of the core studies of concentration. Many students excel in different topics at different rates. Our educational system punishes those students who do not fit the cookie cutter dimensions of a successful student. If the student does not follow the requirements of the educational system, the student will slip through the cracks as the educational system punishes them for making mistakes and failing them for not grasping certain subjects. This process not only breaks the student self-esteem, but also this process hurts students more and more mentally; thus affecting the world. Training students to develop a mindset to not make mistakes stunts their mental growth for developing a millionaire mentality.

I learn the most in life when I make the most mistakes. I have made the transformation in my mind to make as many mistakes as fast as possible. I make many mistakes but I also always learn the lesson. Often I find that I make the same mistakes repeatedly, but eventually I grasp the important lesson, which is the key. Unfortunately, some of my mistakes have cost me thousands of dollars, but I am thankful that I have encountered them because they allow the opportunity to learn valuable lessons and avoid losing millions of dollars in the future.

The day I stop making mistakes is the day that I have reach a plateau in my learning. I challenge myself daily to exercise my mind to find different ways to create wealth. Wealth is everywhere around us, we just need to learn how to recognize the opportunities that come our way.

Many people say that they are not lucky. All the rich people in the world are lucky from some people perspective. The true acronym of LUCK means Laboring Under Correct Knowledge. The problem with many people is that their financial genius is asleep or they are too tired to labor on the opportunities presented. It is not unusual for people to overlook a deal because they do not have the knowledge to take advantage of it.

One of my favorite books of all time is, **The Richest Man in Babylon by George C. Clason.** I want to highlight some of my favorite point on the 5 laws of gold:

> "**Law number 1:** Gold will come gladly and in increasing quantity to any man who puts aside no less than 10% of earnings to create an estate of his future and his family
>
> **Law number 2:** Gold will work diligently and contentedly for the wise owner who finds for it profitable employment multiplying even as the flocks of the field. Gold is an eager employee and is eager to multiply if it given the chance.
>
> **Law number 3:** Gold likes to cling on the protection of the owner who invests it under the advice of men who is wise in its handling. Gold clings to the cautious owner and flees from the careless owner.

Law number 4: Gold slip away from the man who invests it in businesses or purposes for which he is not familiar or not approved by those skilled in its keep.

Law number 5: Gold flees from the man who force it to impossible earnings or who follows the alluring advice of tricksters or schemers or who trusts it in his own inexperience and romantic desires and investments."

I have auto summarized some of the excerpts from the book, The Richest Man in Babylon, and I highly recommend this book for others to read and enjoy. This book should be in everybody's library. These laws in George Clason's book influenced my life and the way I view and handle money today. I owe great credit to the person who recommended this read this book. This book alone will give you a foundation to start building wealth. George Clason has different stories inside of the book to give you a clear picture on how wealth can accumulate.

For example, there was a story about a wealthy man who had a son and wanted to teach him the laws of gold. The wealthy man did not believe in the philosophy of passing the wealth to his heirs just because that was acceptable to society. He wanted to be certain that when he passed away that the gold that he accumulated over the years will continue to thrive through various investments. The wealthy man wanted to be certain that his son new the importance of the five laws of gold and wanted to teach the son a lesson about money. The wealthy man would rather donate his money to different charitable organizations after he passed away than give his money to his heirs who are not wise in its handling. He gave his son a tablet with the five laws of gold written on it, a slave, and a bag of gold. The wealthy man advised his son to go out in the wilderness and report to him in 10 years. If the son returns with the same amount of money, the wealthy man would make his son the head of the estate. The son went off to the wilderness and was very ambitious to make his father proud. The son ignored the laws and focused on the gold. He tried different investment schemes and eventually lost all of his money. The son ended up losing everything that he owned. After the son was broke and faced bitter days, the son finally looked that the tablets his father gave him.

Eventually the son reported to his father on his progress because the 10 years finally arrived. The father set up a big celebration for his arrival and was interested to hear his son story. The father asked if he maintained the money that he left him. The son told him about his adventures and the highlights over the years. The son told him that if he applied the laws of gold it would have saved him grief over the years. The son eventually gave his father double the money and expressed that the laws was more important to him than the gold. The son valued the laws over the gold and told his father that if he had to do it all over again he would rather have the laws of gold. He said that money alone is nothing without the laws. I recommend people to read this book to get more insightful information about money.

I want to give you another tip on how you can start conditioning your mind towards financial success. Stop making negative comments and start asking positive questions. You might be wondering what I mean by this and it is very simple. When you make statements like "I can't do that!" "I am not sure if I can do this!" and "I can't afford it!" You are making negative statements that will limit your thought process and thinking. You need to ask yourself "How can I get this done?" or "How can I afford this?"

When you start asking "How", you are triggering your brain to think and you will begin to notice all of the possibilities to solve problems by asking yourself these questions. This is the main reason this book is entitled "H.O.W?" to open your mind to other possibilities to help generate income.

Once you start asking yourself questions, you are exercising your mind to get creative by opening up your mind to another reality. When you make statements like "I can't do this!" your mind will shut down and will not consider all of the possibilities available. If you look back in history, the idea that humans can fly was never possible but it is now a reality. People are flying across the world and into space because someone had the courage to think outside the box and create a new reality.

True wealth occurs obtained when you remain focused. I hear so many people that put their whole life and savings in the hands of brokers and financial gurus. One of the reasons why they call themselves brokers is because they are usually broke. You should be careful in handing your money to different people without knowing anything about the investment you plan to participate.

It is common that most people put their earnings and savings in the hands of brokers and different mutual fund managers. I will not mention the many companies out there that are preying on innocent people to contribute investments that give people historical data and hidden fees. Personally, I believe that mutual funds are one of the biggest rip-offs in the industry. The main disadvantages that I see are that you do not have control of the performance of your money. If you cannot control your investment, it might be a risky investment.

Control is the reason why the rich get richer. They know how to control, protect, preserve, and invest their money and allow their money to multiply. It might take average person years just to save $20,000.00. The rich have the ability to borrow $20,000.00 in a matter of minutes and invest that money to make a profit and give the money back. This form of leverage is the main secret why the rich stay rich and the poor will always remain poor. Use OPM (Other's People Money) to help increase your wealth and start generating unlimited income now.

Some people who are reading this book might feel that borrowing money is easier said than done and it is difficult for them to do this. We could be in a recession, depression, or in a soaring economy, money will always be available if the opportunity or the deal is right. For instance, I will give you a situation where I do not have the money but I will show you how I created the money to produce more money.

Let us say that I find a piece of property in a recession market that is currently undervalued. I notice that this is a multifamily unit and it is 100% occupied. I look at the leases approved by me. I do not have the money to buy this property because it has an asking price of $40,000.00. I tried to get a loan from the bank, but I do not have the 20% for a down payment. How can I get the money for this deal? I ask myself.

Well, as a licensed real estate agent in the state of Georgia. I market and advertise on www.meetup.com, www.craigslist. com, www.facebook.com, www.myspace.com, or in my local paper and find a partner to help me do this deal. For instance, I post it as a listing "Partner is needed! A Great multifamily is on the market with a positive cash flow. This deal won't last, so contact me at the number below for more details!" You will find it surprising the amount of people who will be interested in this deal. Your goal is to pique the potential partner's interests and give them more details once they are paying attention.

Once I find a partner, I will tell them that I am a licensed real estate agent and I have found a great opportunity, however I do not have all of the money for the down payment. We generate an operating agreement where I will use my real estate commission as part of the down payment and you will use the remainder balance for the down payment. In the business operating agreement, we will split the profits 50/50 and we will dissolve the corporation once we sell the property or keep the corporation to buy other properties and place them in the Real Estate Holding company.

I highly advise that you consult with your legal advisors on this particular strategy; as it is a current practice. I also recommend for people to get their real estate license and use commission as part of your down payment when you closing each transaction. Originally, I wanted to obtain a real estate license as a strategy to use my commission as part of my down payment on properties that I plan to purchase or purchase through my company.

Let me give you an example of the advantage of having a real estate license. Let us say that I find a commercial property with an asking sales price of $1,000,000.00. The question that I always ask myself is, "How can I afford this million dollar property when I have no money in my account?" While I am asking myself this question, I open my mind of the endless possibilities to purchase this deal. I would use my commission as a strategy to secure this deal. I will use this particular strategy because it is the most common strategy that I would use in this particular scenario. I will use my commission as part of my down payment and I will finance the remainder balance using OPM (Other People's Money) from a bank or private investors.

Real Estate commissions are negotiable in the state of Georgia as long as both parties agree on the commission amount. Typically, I will negotiate a minimum of 5% commission of the total sales price but typically not uncommon to ask for 8-10%. My commission on a million dollar property at 5% will be $50,000.00. The banks will usually finance a property if the property has a positive cash flow and if I can come up with at least 20% as a down payment.

You might say to yourself," Well, I don't have the credit and I just filed for bankruptcy a few months back!" "I can't afford to do a million dollar deal!" "This strategy will never work in today's economy!" If you are making these statements, then you should stop and open your mind to transform your reality. You must consider all your options for instance, the banks will give you a non-recourse loan to buy commercial properties. A non-recourse loan does not allow the lender to pursue anything other than collateral, which is the property that you are buying. Your credit is not a major decision factor if the bank is going to give you the money. Banks are willing to giving you the money pending on the cash flow potential from the property that you wish to buy. The building is your credit if you play the commercial property game. Always remember, **"If the deal is right, the money will always be available."** This statement posted on your wall will help with any internal doubts.

Let us say on this property that I wish to purchase, the bank will finance only 75% of the $1,000,000.00 property. I will have to bring $250,000.00 in order for this deal to work. I have identified earlier that I will receive a commission check for $50,0000.00 now I must come up with the other $200,000.00 to make this work. How can I get the $200,000.00 to do this deal? This is a rhetorical question and there is a clear solution to this problem. I tell the seller that I will need him to finance 20% of the loan for 10 years if they want this deal done. But what if the seller doesn't want to owner finance the $200,000.00 portion of the deal? Then I find a cash partner or walk away.

Here is a major tip that people will need to understand. It is not uncommon for sellers to hold back a note on commercial transactions. The RESPA (Real Estate Settlement Procedures Act) laws that are placed in residential transactions do not affect commercial deals. RESPA is about closing costs and settlement procedures. RESPA requires that the consumers receive disclosures at various times in the transaction and outlaws kickbacks that increase the cost of settlement services. In commercial transactions, you can be very creative. The rich play this game every day. Please contact your CPA, and other advisors on the guidelines on commercial and residential properties in your local area.

By using the aforementioned strategy, I have given you a realistic example on how I purchased a $1,000,000.00 property with literally no money out of my pocket. I used my commission and borrowed the rest of the money to do this deal. Deals like this are very common. If you use the concepts from the board game Monopoly, you would learn to buy 4 green houses and turn them into red hotels. You would then be on your way towards financial freedom by investing in real estate alone. You can do all of this without using any of your money. All you need is a positive attitude and strategies to put a deal together. Real Estate has created more millionaires than any industry in the world. It is a simple process. Do you have the discipline to be consistent?

If you want to get rich, start each day by asking yourself, "How can I do more for less?" For those of you who are in a financial bind today, I encourage you to do a little each day for tomorrow. Earn enough to pay off the past; earn a little more for the future.

Remember, you do not need a lot of money to start building your wealth. However, it does require that you use your God-given resources to make the most of every precious day. Create your future today, not tomorrow. Incorporate The Four Stages of Learning towards financial freedom and practice some of the suggestions in this book.

CHAPTER

I can't believe it's not MONEY?
Money is an idea that can be easily created....

Money is not necessarily wealth, but only the result of wealth. Wealth is measured by time not in money. Wealth is the amount of time you can survive without you physically working. If I told you that money is not real, how would you respond? Anything can be called "MONEY" if everybody agrees that it is money. History tells us that England used Talley sticks as a form of currency and they considered it legal tender. The king will cut certain amount of sticks and engrave them with different markings and depending on the size will determine the denomination. Fast-forwarding to the future, instead of using sticks as a form of US currency we use green paper called fiat money. Ironically, when people say money does not grow on trees, technically it does.

The industry standard always used Gold and silver as the true form of currency. People started using fiat money aka "paper money", because it is accessible and a lot easier to carry instead of walking around with gold and silver. People around the world acknowledge that gold and silver is the universal standard form of currency.

The Rich transform their ideas into cash. They use this cash and generate assets by using Other Peoples' Money (OPM). Consider this as one of the most powerful statements in this book.

True money is just an idea; one that is created in the mind. As I mentioned earlier, sticks considered money were considered legal tender. The true question that you should ask yourself is "How can I use my ideas and create legal tender to buy assets?" I believe that Robert Kiyosaki said it best when he said, "Assets FEED you and Liabilities EAT you."

Money is a necessary tool that we all need. Regardless of the type of currency or the name you call it, money is a major factor for survival. Depending how much money you generate, money will determine the house, car, clothes, food, and lifestyle you have. Money is up there with oxygen, you need it to live. Once you become a master over money instead of a slave, you will see the world differently and notice that the world has too much money.

Money is an idea and anybody can create it as long as he or she develops the ideas in the mind. Everybody has a million dollar idea but sometimes it might require a lot of thinking and creativity to bring that idea to life. I can remember when the slinky entered the market and all the children wanted to have one. This metal spring did not have a lot design or major graphics and it was simple. The children loved this and it was an overnight success.

You can see products all over the world and many of the products are good ideas and inventions. However, the idea alone is not enough to start creating money. You will need a mission behind the idea and a team of people to help deliver the product to the masses. I recommend that you read Rich Dad's Guide to Investing by Robert Kiyosaki. This is a necessary read and Robert educates readers the additional steps needed once you have that idea and will give you a guide to investing.

The good thing about ideas is that you have the option of making it a reality. Once you have your idea, protect your ideas because they are more valuable than money. One creative idea can make you richer than you can ever imagine. You want to do something one time and reap the benefits year after year. For example, when you buy an investment property with little or no money down, you close on that transaction one time but you are reaping from the initial investment year after.

Musicians, writers, and movie stars receive residual royalty checks by doing something only once. The rich are willing to take the time to do something once and continue producing income year after year. This is a critical difference from a poor person and a rich person.

If you are an employee, you must continuously do work in order to be paid. The moment you stop working will be the moment when your income stream will be dries up. It is critical that you generate other streams of income in addition to your paycheck from your job. The problem with being an employee is that you are chasing something that is not real, because money is not real. The best illustration that I can give is of a man is riding a donkey with a carrot placed in front of the donkey. The donkey chases the illusion while the man is getting to the destination or has the opportunity to fulfill his dreams. In the end, the donkey might never get the carrot the power will always be in the hands of the rider.

This is primarily the reason why the rich do not work for money; they have their money work for them. If you are an employee and you are working for only one stream of income, then you might want to consider some of the tips in this book and start having money work for you. What will you do if your job is phased out? What will you do if you are laid off or fired? What will you do if you work for a company 19 years and they fire you just before you hit retirement eligibility from your company? What will you do if you cannot immediately find employment for months?

Always ask yourself questions and trigger your mind to think. There is an old saying that goes, "A mind is a terrible thing to waste!" Challenge yourself constantly by inquiring about different issues in the world. Everybody has the possibility to generate endless amount of money if you start asking yourself "How can I do it?" Asking yourself, "How can I do it, triggers your mind and force it to think of endless of possibilities to get it done. When you say, "I CAN"T do it!" You are making a statement that what you believe is true and your mind will not think of possible solutions.

My mentor has mentioned several times that there are three types of incomes. The three incomes are: earned income, portfolio income, and passive income. Earned income is income that you get when you work for the money. This type of income is earned **when you work for the money.** You usually will receive a paycheck from your employer and get a W2 form at the end of the year. Portfolio income is income that you generate when **you put your money to work** like in the stock market. The third type of income is passive income. This type of income is earned when your money is working for you without you being there. This type of income is usually from Real Estate, royalties from books, music, and other streams. To get a more in-depth insight on these types of income I would highly recommend that you go to www.richdad.com and join his community and increase your income by learning.

The problem of having earned income, a "JOB", is that you have limited to no control of your income. Your pay is usually set and you are hit the hardest on your share of tax. This stream of income will be considered risky in my eyes because you have limited and no control of this income. Many people will disagree with me but the people who just recently been laid-off might agree with me. As we approach tough economic times and volatility in the economy, having earned income as your only stream of income your financial days may get a little cloudy. Regardless of the economy, people will always get laid-off, so I will always classify earned income as risky.

Some of the biggest investments that many people make are in their job. Investing in your job is fine if you do not want to control your asset. People are usually comfortable investing towards making other people rich instead of investing in approved assets that will help them generate increasing wealth. It is always wise to keep a portion of your money every month for investing. You don't want to be the one to lose your only stream of income without cash reserves.

Many people feel that earned income is the safest income classification out there, because they work for their money and receive a paycheck after a long days work. This may appear very attractive, but it is the most risky form of income to generate. Though I am not making a recommendation for you to quit your job, there are ways to prepare for job loss. If you decide to quit your job, you should ensure at least 6-12 months of cash reserves are available.

Before you quit your job, you first should ensure that you have at least 6 to 12 months of cash reserves in your bank. This is very important if you are going to make the transition from an employee to an employer. This will allow you to cover your daily expenses and liabilities that you have generated over time.

CHAPTER 3

Who stole your Money?
The numbers will tell you the story...

I will give you a brief history on money that many people might not know about. If you do not learn the lessons from the past, you are doomed to repeat it. Recessions and depressions only exists because of the Central Bankers manipulate the flow of money and the money supply. Economists and other agencies will explain that recessions and depressions are a natural part of the "Business cycle" and this is far from the case. People are aware of the depressions and recessions but many people truly do not understand why this is taking place. After reading this chapter you might know more about money and economics compared to analysts that appear on Television or (Tell) (Lies) (visually). Central Bankers want to ensure that they control more money, which will leave less money for the average person.

This book's sole intention is to open your mind and get you to see that money do grow on trees and can be easily accessible if you have the ideas. Do not accept any information presented to you without first checking it out for yourself. I encourage all of my readers to verify all of information in this book and start asking, "How can I obtain wealth within 30 days by using some or all of the strategies presented?" Constantly ask yourself what are the other ways I can generate income not mentioned in this book. There are millions of ways to generate income. All it takes is one good idea and a system. This book is only a reference and a guide, but you hold the keys to your destiny. With the power of the Internet, anything is possible, and everybody has the chance to obtain true wealth and pass it on generations after your lifetime.

To get a true understanding on money, you must understand the definition of a moneychanger. A moneychanger is a trade involving exchanges of coins in different denomination. It is the origin of modern banking in Europe. I will refer the "Banking System" as the "moneychangers", so you can get a better understanding on who stole your money! After all, this is the title of this chapter. I am sure there will be mixed feelings on this chapter, but I am an educator and I plan to do just that. The information might shock some people, but you can use this information as a strategy to help you with your journey to build endless wealth for you and your family. There is an old saying, "Don't hate the PLAYER, hate the GAME!" Obtaining wealth is like a game, if you want to play you have to know the rules.

You can find most of the information in this chapter by reading some or all of the books listed below or doing your own research on the Internet.

The Life of William Ewart Gladstone,	John Moreley
Secrets of the Federal Reserve,	Eustace Mullins
The Great crash 1929,	John Gailbraith
F.D.R. My Exploited Father-In-Law,	Curtis B. Dall
The Creature from Jekyll Island,	G. Edward Griffin
The Money Changers,	Patrick Carmack

I encourage people to read some or all of the books presented in this book if you want to know more about the banking system and who stole your money. I encourage people to read some or all of the books presented in this book. I have to give credit to the authors I mentioned throughout this book. Their information and research inspired me to write this book. Again, this book is only a guide to get more in depth information on wealth I encourage everyone to have a library on the subject. My ultimate goal in life is to help wake up as many people up as possible towards financial freedom.

The banking system, aka "money changers" have been around for many years and played different roles in many religions and throughout society. The banking system became more sophisticated over the years and grew rapidly. The concept of lending money and charging people high interest rates from the money they never had was usury and they camouflaged the high interest concept in the Catholic Church and other organizations. Some leaders tried to stop this usury practice but the banking system always find their way back into society. Many people do not research and ask why we need the banking system and why they want to play an active role in society. The answer to this question is Control and Unlimited Power.

Julius Caesar fought against the moneychangers and minted coins to benefit all of the people. He "created" a large supply of money, produced jobs for people, and initiated a thriving economy. The people loved him for this and cherished his concept. The moneychangers hated him for doing this and they were the main plot of his assignation. Another great figure that stood up against the moneychangers was Jesus Christ. Jesus Christ began his 3-½ year ministry in Jerusalem by driving the corrupt moneychangers from the temple. In the last year of his life, he used physical force to throw the moneychangers out of the temple. This was the only time in his ministry that he used physical force against anyone. He knew the corruption that the moneychangers were causing in the temple. Therefore, he hated this concept and tried to abolish it.

The Jews came to Jerusalem to pay their temple tax, but they only could pay it with a special coin, the half-shekel. This is equivalent to a ½ ounce of pure silver. It was the only coin at that time that was assured weight and without the image of a pagan Emperor. The Jews thought the half-shekel was only acceptable to GOD because it was a form of currency and did not have any images on it. Since the moneychangers had majority of the shekels it caused a huge demand because only a few was in circulation. Therefore, the moneychangers raised the price of the half-shekel to whatever the market could bear. They monopolized the currency and made exorbitant profits and forcing the Jews to pay the money changers anything they demanded. Jesus recognized what the money changers were doing and ran the money changers away from the Temple.

As you can see, I have mentioned two most influential leaders that tried to stop the moneychangers and the usury concept, yet they still find their way to return in our society right under our eyes. In year 1024, the moneychangers had control of Medieval England's money supply and this era known as goldsmiths, which was the birth of the Fractional Reserve Banking System that we know about today. Paper money began as a receipt after depositing gold with a goldsmith. To simplify the process, the bearer makes the receipts rather than to the individual depositor, making it readily transferable without the need for signature.

Eventually, the goldsmiths realized that only a fraction of depositors ever came in and demanded their gold at any one time, so they found a way to cheat people and manipulate gold. They started issuing more receipts than they had gold. This concept fueled the moneychangers greed and they discovered how to slither back into society and found an easier way to make money hand over fists without people realizing their strategy. As they gradually grew more confident on how they can manipulate the people, they would lend out up to 10 times the amount they had in their deposits.

This concept was just an "idea" to create more money. Remember what I mentioned earlier that money is an "idea" and only an idea. I am not recommending that you use the particular idea that the moneychangers used to monopolize the monetary system. I want to show you how a simple idea can change your finances almost overnight and how to play the game.

The moneychangers discovered how to control the money supply and know how to truly create a depression, recession, or a booming economy. This is the major reason why we have depressions, because the moneychangers found a way to tighten the money supply and depress the economy almost overnight. This gives the banking system total control and absolute power of the world monetary system. Inflation is the reduction in worth of money borne by the common person; this is due to the economy being flooded with too much money.

For example, let us say that 5 billion dollars is in active circulation in the United States. The banks will print out additional 15 billion dollars in addition to the 5 billion dollars. They will print out the extra paper to overflow the money supply and lend that money that never existed through bank loans to the consumers. That will reduce the initial 5 billion dollars in circulation value and no gold to back up the additional money in circulation. If you look at it in a form of a percentage you will see that the initial 5 billion dollars in circulation is only 25% of the money supply and the banks magical money that they created of 15 billion dollars is the 75% money supply that they control. Now they control majority the money in circulation with no questions asked from the public.

Therefore, to inflate the economy, the moneychangers just release more money to the people and the value of the currency will begin to plummet; thus creating inflation. Why would the moneychangers create inflation? It is simple to create more money and wealth by bankrupting the economy and controlling governments and nations because they will have to borrow more money to climb their way out of debt and will be forever indebted to the banking system. It is like borrowing from Peter to pay Paul theory. Themoneychangers or the "Bankers" just wait for the people to go bankrupt, seize, and capitalize the true assets like real estate, businesses, and even our government. It is amazing to hear that America is in billions or if not trillions of dollars in debt to the moneychangers. As the common person's money diminishes in worth the people will go to the bank to get more loans from the banks and the banks will charge ridiculous interest rates just to use the magical money to buy basic necessities. Inflation never affects a central bank; in fact, they are the only group who can benefit from it. If the economy is short of money, they can simply print more. Now through the power of the Internet and technology, they can wire funds without wasting paper. This allows the central banks to create money faster. You can get more information on whole banking system online or reading the books I have mentioned.

How did the moneychangers in England come to America? Well, you must return to 1764 when the Bank of England officials ask Benjamin Franklin about the rapid prosperity of the American colonies.

Benjamin Franklin quoted, *"That is simple In the Colonies we issue our own money. It is called **Colonial Scrip**. We issue it in proper proportion to the demands of trade and industry to make the products pass easily from the producers to the consumers. In this manner creating for ourselves our own paper money, we **CONTROL** its purchasing power, and we have no interest to no one."*

The British Parliament instantly passed the Currency Act of 1764. This Act prohibited colonial officials from issuing their own money and ordered them to pay all future taxes in gold or silver coins.

In response to this, Benjamin Franklin wrote in his autobiography:

"In one year, the conditions were so reversed that the era of prosperity ended, and a depression set in, to such an extent that the streets of the colonies were filled with the unemployed...The colonies would gladly have borne the little tax on tea and other matters had it not been that England took away from the colonies their money which created unemployment and dissatisfaction."

The viability of the colonists to get power to issue their own money permanently out of the hands of King George III and the international bankers was the prime reason for the revolution war.

I hope that this information will give you an understanding on why we live in a volatile economy. Ten Percent of people control 90% of the money, while the 90% of the people fights for survival for 10% of the money in circulation. Everyone still has the power to become wealthy. You just have to understand the game and understand how to play the game with existing rules Do not work for money! This is the rule that many rich people understand. As you can see, money is only an idea and a concept that someone created. Working for it will delay you from getting wealthy.

Always put your money to work and reinvest your profits in assets that will generate money, thus putting your money to work. The faster you understand this concept and create money from your ideas; the faster you will acquire as much power as the Central Bankers that created money legally and generated endless cash from ideas, concepts, and inventions.

Since I understand the rules of the game, I am now I am ready to play. In the second quarter of 2009, I purchased a duplex near a college community in Atlanta for $8,000.00. Personally, the cash was not readily available in my account since I keep my money moving through different investments. I purchased this property using a micro-loan from a bank. This property was a foreclosed property that I found in a real estate database. I had an advantage because I am a licensed real estate agent with exclusive privilege in the multiple listing databases in the state of Georgia. Since this was a cash purchase I needed proof of funds in my account when I submit the offer to the bank. Instantly the money was readily available in my account within 30 minutes from the bank loan. I do not worry about the debt I just created since it gives me a passive income stream. I found this deal when economists say that we are in a recession. I purchased this property placed two tenants in the property and now I control a real estate parcel; thus generating a passive income stream from the money that I just created. The faster you are able to create money the richer you will become.

CHAPTER

How did I get a "mort" - "gage"?
The engagement until death...

"The word "mortgage": It seemeth that the cause why it is called mortgage is, for that it is doubtful whether the Feoffor will pay at the day limited such summe or not, & if he doth not pay, then the Land which is put in pledge upon condition for the payment of the money, is taken from him for ever, and so dead to him vpon condition, &c. And if he doth pay the money, then the pledge is dead as to the Tenant, &c."

The great jurist Sir Edward Coke (1552-1634)

Mortgages have been around since England in the year 1190 AD. "Mort" is a Latin word that means "Death" and "Gage" is from the sense of that word to pledge or agree to forfeit. The simplest breakdown of this word "Mortgage" is **the engagement until death or a death contract.**

In America, we are conditioned as far back as the early 1900s to enter in this engagement until death. When the European settlers came to America, they brought these ideas and principles from England, and early Americans adopted this engagement as a way of life.

In the early 1900s, not everyone was able to engage in the death contract because the qualifications were extreme. The main requirements were for you to put at least 50% of your money as a down payment and you only had 5 years to pay the rest of the balance. You can only imagine how extreme it was to enter in this death contract. I only wonder how many people would qualify for mortgages, if the same requirements applied today.

Well, this engagement standard continued through The Great Depression. When President Franklin D. Roosevelt came into office, he had lowered the standard for more people to participate into the death contract. His administration introduced a creative concept to make it will be more enticing for Americans. In 1934, the Federal Housing Administration (FHA) was born. FHA was created to insure mortgage lenders against losses from default. Now the risk had been taken away from the lenders and they were motivated to have as many people as possible to enter into a death contract because they had the insurance from the government to back these contracts.

The FHA also developed the 30-year fixed-rate loan program. This gave the homeowners in America lower monthly payments and lowered the down payment requirement to participate in the death contract. This worked for a while, but the problem started to arise when the lenders "the producers" were running out of money for the people "the consumers".

The definition of "consume" is a person or thing that consumes until there is nothing left. A consumer is like a parasite. It eats away until there is nothing left. It also means a heterotrophic organism that ingests other organisms or organic matter in a food chain. I wonder why other countries see Americans in general as consumers and not producers.

The US government was forced into a position to "bail-out" the falling economy. This is like déjà vu in the early 21st century with the "bail-out" issues and the volatile economy that we are facing today. Private lenders were running out of money to lend to people and they needed a place to turn for help. They figured their big "Uncle" could help with their shortfalls. In 1938, to make more death contracts available for the consumers, the government created the Federal National Mortgage Association (FNMA), better known as Fannie Mae. This entity bought FHA-insured loans and sold them as securities on the financial stock markets. This process allowed the lenders aka "producers" to keep the pool of mortgage-lending funds full, in effect, to the buyers aka "consumers".

What are the long-term effects of this creative strategy produced by the government? This made it easier for consumers to engage in the contract and as long as the government keeps insuring these notes, the lenders will continue to offer these death contracts to the masses. Now that lenders are going to a central source for their money, loan terms, interest rates, and underwriting guidelines are in one accord.

The only requirement that the lenders had was to follow Fannie Mae's guidelines and restrictions if they wanted to sell their loans to the secondary market. This seemed like a "win-win" situation, but what is the long term affects?

The mortgage game revamped itself as we coast through the future to the WWII era. Soldiers were ready to purchase homes after the war and they became avid consumers that were motivated to buy homes. The war veterans were creating a booming economy and demanding mortgages. Because of the soldiers were avid consumers and helped with the booming economy, the government had to think of another creative plan. In 1944, the Veterans Administration, (a similar program to the FHA), received the right to "guarantee" the mortgage loans made by private lenders, but this time to veterans that served in this era. Now the lenders had the "insurance" from FHA and the "guarantee" from the government to secure the loans, the lenders are covered regardless of the outcome of the consumer. The VA program made it easier for veterans to buy a home because the veteran would not need a down payment to purchase a home. The demand for the death contracts was high and the mortgage industry soared.

As I go on through the history of the death contracts, you will see how it gradually becomes acceptable in our lives. In 1938, the Canadian government introduced the National Housing Act (NHA). The Parliament of Canada passed the National Housing Act in this year. This program intended to promote the construction of new houses, the repair and modernization of existing houses, and the improvement of housing and living conditions. This Act amended in 1985 and 1999. In 1954, the NHA followed the American footsteps by ensuring the death contracts in their country. It is very interesting how the death contracts spread to different nations and geared as many people as possible to fall for this scam. The Amendment of the Bank Act in Canada allowed charter banks to lend money for mortgages. The mortgage industry lowered the standards to allow as many people as possible to get into death contracts. The baby boomers that entered the workforce, including women, and double-income families were typical. Before the baby boomers entered the workforce, one stream of income was good enough for a family to survive. Higher income levels propelled higher spending. With reality, there was a larger demand on expensive homes. Such a phenomenon fueled the mortgage industry.

In 1970, the US Congress chartered the Federal Home Loan Mortgage Corporation (FHLMC), better known as Freddie Mac, to increase the supply of mortgage funds available to commercial banks, savings and loan institutions, credit unions, and other mortgage lenders; thus making more funds available to more Americans in this era.

In the 1950s, and 1960s, the typical mortgage terms were between 20-30 years. However, the 1970s the interest rates rose rapidly and the system did an adjustment. The death contracts were reduced to one, three, or five year-terms. Although the 5-year mortgages were rare in the 1980s the interest rates jumped to 21%. As you can see, mortgages grew into a monster that people could not stop. Participating in this concept will keep you poor unless you enter into these contracts with the intentions to have a subcontract if you plan to rent your house to generate income.

The death contracts are constantly changing but the players are still the same. You will have the private lenders giving out the money and the government will insure payment to the lenders get paid regardless of the consumer performance. This cartel has been in existence for many years and I envision that this cartel will continue in years to come. Once you study the history you can forecast what the future will be like. One of the latest developments the mortgage industry created was the Home Equity Lines of Credit. HELOC allowed the homeowner to borrow against the value of the house to receive a line of credit or monthly payments. New programs are constantly created to entice more consumers to enter into these contracts. This allowed more people to get available funds; however, people are not getting this cash to produce more assets, they are consuming all of the money towards liabilities.

People had all of the opportunities in the world to capitalize on these opportunities to leverage from the banks giving mentality. The rich capitalize on concept and using the banks money to create more money. For this reason, it is important to increase your financial intelligence so you can see opportunities and capitalize on them. Regardless of the direction of the economy, you can use these death contracts to your advantage if you know how to play the game. There are all kinds of possibilities when it comes to creating cash flow. The mortgage industry is constantly creating variations to these contracts and entices the consumers, but you want to take these opportunities and become a cash flow producer.

The next chapter will give you more information on how you can capitalize and generate wealth in Real Estate. While people are running around looking for death contracts, the rich are finding ways to build wealth. The rich makes tremendous amount of money when the economy is going in a downward spiral. Take advantage of the opportunities in a rough economy and seize the opportunity to become a producer and not a consumer. Consumerism is inevitable in a capitalistic society. Producers need consumers and consumers need producers. (i.e. Supply and demand) Therefore, if you do consume ensure that the benefits are considered.

CHAPTER 5

How to produce wealth in Real Estate?
The foundation to wealth building...

The one thing about real estate investing is that it's a "learn as you go" business. You do not need to be an expert in every area to start investing in real estate. The more knowledge you have, the easier it will be to solve people's problems. You can specialize in a particular area, but you should have knowledge in all areas. The more knowledge you know, the easier it will be to notice opportunities and take advantage of them as they come your way. It is good to have a real estate agent on your team to help you analyze the real estate deal. Seek advice from real estate agents that personally have income producing real estate in their portfolio. If you are a new investor, start your real estate investing in the residential area. These deals might be smaller than commercial, but this is a great place to start. My first investment property that I purchased was a residential property that was cash flowing $200.00 a month. I bought my first investment property without using my personal cash before I bought my primary residence. America is on sale and it is time that you begin shopping. Many people are running away from real estate because of the media press that doom and gloom talks in the real estate market. The current financial crisis and recent housing bubble burst left many people leery of jumping into the real estate market. However, multitudes of investors around the world are making fortunes in the current real estate market. The people who understand the basics of real estate investing will reap great dividends in the future.

The number one mistake new investors make is paying too much for a property. If you pay too much for a property, there is little to do to correct the problem. The most important thing you must learn if you are investing in real estate is to learn how to determine the value of properties and how to analyze every deal. Do not buy real estate without first looking at the numbers and determining the NET income. Do not make the mistake of many new investors by getting emotional attached to the property. At times, emotions can cloud your vision in rationality. Just because the deal looks great on the surface, does not mean that it is. There is a good chance that a property that can be a financial disaster on your financial statement. For example, when you buy a property you should ask yourself a few questions about the deal. Depending on the answers you have the option to walk away or continue with the deal. Before you purchase the property you should factor vacancy rate, taxes, insurance, Home Owners Association, new developments, managements, and so on. Just because you currently make money on the property the situation might change in the future. I want to leave you with a tip. If you can handle the worst case scenario, consider doing the deal!

In this chapter, I will talk more about tax liens, foreclosures, and commercial properties. You can reap huge dividends if you focus your efforts in these areas in real estate. A piece of real estate is a piece of real estate. In order for you to be successful in real estate, you must know how to analyze the deal or have someone analyze it for you.

It is a good idea to have a team that will help in your journey towards financial freedom and success. If you are the smartest person in your team, you are in trouble. Surround yourself with people who are smarter than you are and always have a mentor by your side. Real Estate is the foundation of wealth and I highly recommend that you consider this strategy to build tremendous amount of financial success.

1. Tax Lien/Deed Opportunities

The one thing that you cannot run away from is TAX. You are taxed when you are born, while you are living, and when you die. This inevitable process will not end unless the government changes this procedure. The tax rate may fluctuate but the process will not end. Taxes are a price you will pay to live in a civilized society. Taxes are collected to assist for salaries, services, and government obligations to live in a civilized society.

Real Estate tax is a way to support your local counties in financial matters. If you believe that you are the only one that owns your home, think again. If you fail to pay for your real estate tax, you will see who the true owner of your home is. Investing in Tax sales opens the opportunity to gain wealth.

Each state may be different on how to invest in Tax lien/ Deed Opportunities so do your due diligence to see what the procedures are in your area. Many taxing jurisdictions use this alternative method of collecting delinquent real estate property taxes. Taxes always become the FIRST lien holder of every property.

TLC's (Tax Lien Certificates) could yield very high rates of returns on your investment when the property is redeemed. You may receive yields as high as 20% per annum or even more. Investing in TLC's would be a very conservative investment that you want additional options instead of the stock market and money market accounts. When you invest in different strategies, always consider your ROI (Return On Investment). The simplified meaning of ROI is the rate you can get your money back from your initial investment.

You can purchase TLC's as low as $500.00 and as high as $50,000.00 depending on the property. In the event the delinquent property owner does not redeem within the time provided for redemption, the holder of the tax lien can receive title to the property.
The ROI on this strategy is infinite. You can invest as little as $500.00 and you can have a property that is worth $100,000.00 once you obtain possession.

Consider that state laws are different and might require additional obligations from you. Please consult with your financial advisors and legal professionals to see how this strategy could work for you. This is a good strategy to use if you looking for a very conservative investment with an astronomical rate of return.

Usually, your local county's courthouse steps holds tax auctions on the first Tuesday of every month. It is a good idea to go a few months just to see how the process works. When I started investing in Tax liens, I went a few times just to get a feel on the bidding process and the concept. I was a rookie on the overall process at one point in time, but after a few months of going and figuring out the process. I became a pro. Do not bid on any properties without your due diligence and without any money. Depending on your state and Local County, payment in full is usually required within a few hours. Once you bid you must buy and the county takes this very serious.

You can find a list of properties that are for auction in your local paper and the listing posted every week on the Friday's paper. It is your local paper that you will find these deals and not the national paper in circulation. Once you identified the properties that you wish to purchase you would see a starting bid next to the property that is auctioned. It is highly recommended that you research the property and see if this would be a good investment prior to the bidding date. Remember you will see only limited people participating at these auctions, but the investors that participate already know the properties that they wish to purchase and you might be bidding against someone who has many cash reserves for the properties. Do not get discouraged as I am sure you will find a deal that is for you.

It is extremely important that you physically look at the property before placing a bid. Some properties or land lots are bad investments because they might have restrictions and will limit you to place a structure on the land or improve the land. Always physically go the address and see what you are buying before you start bidding on the lot. The United States is still under the Queen System with regard to taxes.

All taxes go to the Queen, her heirs, and successors, and throughout the Crown. It began in 1773 in the time of the Boston Tea Party took place. King George III and his government looked to taxing the American colonies as a way of recouping their war costs. They were also looking for ways to reestablish control over the colonial governments that had become independent while the "Crown" was distracted by the war. Royal ineptitude compounded the problem. A series of actions including the Stamp Act (1765), the Townsend Acts (1767) and the Boston Massacre (1770) agitated the colonists, straining relations with England. However, the attempt to tax tea that spurred fired up the colonists and revved up the American Revolution. The "Crown" assumed that the colonists would rather pay the taxes than deny themselves the pleasure of a teacup. The parliament's ploy did not fool the colonists.

We still have demonstrations and protests on taxes and the whole concept on taxes. Regardless of your opinion on taxes, you still have to pay taxes on the land that you own. This is a great investment to start generating income if you are investing on tax lien properties. Even with tax liens, we have the laws of risk and return at work. If the taxpayer continues to make payments of tax and penalties, then the investor is compensated for the risk they took. If payments stop, then the investor (YOU) has collateral (The Property itself), which can be sold off to satisfy the lien.

Keep in mind that tax lien investing is not a new idea. Investors have been doing this for years and it was a great way to purchase properties literally pennies on the dollar. There will be real competition for properties are in excellent conditions or in a great location. Selling these same properties are likely before foreclosure ever takes place. That is still good for the investor because their lien would be satisfied at sale. In Georgia, the owner of the property has a redemption period to pay the taxes, interests, fees, within 12 months and days later. This gives the owner an additional opportunity to pay the taxes. If the property taxes are not paid or the redemption period has expired, you are able to take procession of the property. Please consult with an attorney on the laws on your state and the process to convert the tax certificate into a warranty deed.

This is a great way to get a piece of property for pennies on the dollar and you could have an investment vehicle that is giving you a ROI over 20% or more in real estate. Your

ROI (Return On Investment) in this strategy is more than you would obtain from investing in a Mutual Fund, CD, or in your savings account. You could get a higher ROI if you did technical investing in the stock market but I will get into that in chapter 8 in this book. This is a good place to start if you have the money for the minimum bid for the property. People are always asking me what a good ROI is when investing. I always respond that I try to obtain a minimum of 15% ROI in my first year. If I am investing in real estate, I always strive for 45% ROI or more in my first year. I want to keep my money moving in every investment vehicle that I participate in. I want my money to be in and out and re-invest my profits repeatedly. The higher the ROI the faster I will get my money from my initial investment and keep it flowing.

Multiple streams of income are very important and will be a requirement for survival. If you are depending on Social Security alone, you are in trouble. Be prepared to see the gap widen the rich and the poor in the near future. "Would you rather be rich or poor? The choice is yours?" Only you will know the answer to this question. If you are striving to be rich, then you want to keep you money moving and invest in cash flow producing assets. Investing in Tax liens/ Certificates is a good place to start for the savvy and/or beginner investor.

2. Foreclosed/Auction Opportunities

Real estate is a volatile industry. Foreclosures are inevitable in any market condition. Since this market is volatile, you have a tremendous opportunity to participate in real estate. You can find these opportunities through the Internet, real estate agent, your local paper, and notable attorneys.

Public records usually place foreclosed homes in their ads and this information is easily accessible. This strategy is recommended for experienced investors and people who truly understand how the real estate game really works.

Foreclosure is the legal process by which a borrower in default under a mortgage is deprived of his/her interest in the mortgaged property. Many people will face foreclosure regardless of the economic situation. This strategy is a good way to capitalize from homes that are in default. Banks are willing to auction these properties at a discounted price to reduce the loss that the banks encounter.

You may face several pitfalls when investing in foreclosed properties. This strategy is recommended for people who might have the lump sum to purchase these discounted properties. A large amount of cash reserves might be required when you participate in these auctions. You might also find that you need additional funds to repair or rehab the property to make it a beneficial investment. However, you can make huge profits if you have access to the large amount of cash to afford these properties.

Always keep in mind that greater the risk, the greater the reward. This strategy is not for the beginner investor. This strategy, if done correctly, will benefit you financially in order of magnitudes. You can make tremendous amounts of profits if you buy low and sell high at market price.

Lets say that the market value of the home is worth $100,000.00, and you bought this property for $35,000.00, the profit margin is unbelievable. This is a great strategy; however, this is my least favorite. When you look into an investment, always consider what will be your cash flow potential when making a financial decision. I do not like to have a lot of money tied up in a particular investment.

When you buy a fore closed home, you might do either one of three things. You 1 1ay buy it, fix it up, and sell the home. This process is also k nown as "Flipping". You may buy the house and use it as 1 rental property. You also might just buy these properties and use it as a personal residence.

This strategy is good when the economist indicate that the market is down. Always remember that the real estate market is volatile and keep in mind that you want to buy low and sell high. Be very careful where you get your financial advice. Many people ask financial questions from their broke neighbors, family, or friends. Always protect your money and invest it under the advice of people who are wise in its handling. Money clings to the cautious owner and flees from the careless owner.

Buying REOs (Real Estate Owned) is a good strategy but remember to keep cash reserves aside for repairs. Usually, these homes might have excessive wear and tear and might need some TLC. I would recommend this investment for the experienced real estate investor because you might buy a property at a reduced price but you might pay more out of your pocket from costly repairs. It is a good idea to get a home inspector to help you determine if the home will be a good buy. It will save you money in the long run and prevent from unwanted surprises after you buy them.

3. Get the land under the business

Real Estate should always be in your financial portfolio. Every wealthy person has or controls some type of real estate in their financial statement. Personally, real estate has always been my primary choice of investment. My next favorite type of investment is the stock market. I enjoy making money in the stock market when the market goes up, down, or sideways. I will give you some tips on the type of technical investment strategies that I currently do in the stock market.

Get the land under the business. This strategy is my favorite in the real estate game. I am a licensed real estate agent in the state of Georgia and this strategy is helpful if you have a good real estate agent. I recommend that you contact a real estate agent to assist you in this strategy. You want to get a real estate agent who specializes in commercial properties. Investing in commercial properties is the fastest way to build wealth. If you have personal credit problems, then this strategy is for you. When you are investing in commercial real estate, your personal credit score is not very important. Bankers and lenders are looking at the potential income that the property can generate when furnishing out loans for commercial properties and not your personal credit score. This is called a "non-recourse loan". Non-recourse debt typically finances commercial real estate and similar projects with high capital expenditures, long loan periods, and uncertain revenue streams.

Commercial properties will allow you to build wealth faster in comparison to residential properties. However, it is wise that beginner investors start in the residential real esate market. Study this concept when you play the famous family board game like monopoly. You buy 4 green houses and 1 red hotel. The person that has the most hotels on properties on the game usually wins. The green houses are a representation of the residential properties and the red hotels are an indicator of the commercial properties. The color "red" indicates that these properties are "RED HOT".

I will give you a great tip on where to find these commercial properties in the newspaper. You can find properties in your local newspaper in the Business Section. **This is a good place to find potential partners,** established businesses for sale, and commercial properties. This tip alone is a great place to start if you have plans on investing in commercial properties. I personally recommend that you invest in areas where you live or areas that are not too far from your primary residence. You can find great deals in Texas, but if you live in Hawaii, then I highly recommend that you avoid investments out of your reach.

I will explain the 4 green houses (residential) and 1 red Hotel (commercial) concept and how it works in reality. If you are a being investor, I will present a strategy on how to build wealth in real estate on a 10 year plan. You buy a duplex, triplex, or a quaduplex as a primary residence instead of a single-family home. Duplexes, triplexes, and quaduplexes, are still considered residential properties and you can qualify for some of the first-time homebuyer programs that Fannie Mae or Freddie Mac have to offer. I know that rules and regulations change constantly so I would consult with a professional lender who is familiar with these programs or new programs that may be available for you.

One of our biggest expenses next to taxes is what we spend for rent or mortgage. For illustrative purposes, only I will say that the average rent is $1,000.00 a month. Depending on your area, this average could be low or high. If I purchase a duplex as a primary residence, I will live in one of the units and I will rent out the other for the price of what I would pay for my mortgage. As long as I keep a tenant in the other unit, basically I would be living rent-free. Lets say that I am able to keep a tenant in the other unit for at least 2 years. I would have generated $24,000.00 of passive income and I can reinvest this $24,000.00 in another multifamily home, move out of my current unit, and live in another multifamily unit. I would   replace the unit that I was staying in with a tenant that is willing to pay $1000.00 a month for rent. Now this is where it can start getting exciting. In a perfect world I would have a duplex that is 100% occupied and I am getting a gross income stream of $2,000.00 a month from my first (green) house. I am living in my second multi-family unit this time; I buy a triplex or a 3 unit apartment building. Depending on the market conditions in real estate market, I find a triplex that has an asking price of $120,000.00. I would spend my $24,000.00 as 20% downpayment to purchase this property.

Depending on the market conditions and your credit worthiness or your business, you can get financing if you put at least 20% for the down payment on investment properties. If you are disciplined enough you would have the 20% down payment without any costs from you. I will duplicate the same system on my triplex. I will charge $1000.00 a month for rent for both of my units. I will have an income stream of $4000.00 a month from both of my units combined. I will stay in my triplex for 2 years and purchase another unit from the profits I have generated from my tenants. In a perfect world, I would have accumulated $96,000.00 of passive income from my first and second green house. I hope you are starting to see the trend.

My third investment, I would purchase another multifamily unit. Depending on the amount of money you wish to put down will determine the percentage of the down payment on the property. I will decide to only use $25,000.00 as a down payment and keep the other $71,000.00 for other investments or working capital for a business. Again, I would use the $25,000.00 as a down payment on a $125,000.00 property. Now I have three multi-family units (green houses) that I am getting a positive income stream every month.

This time I have found a great deal. I buy a quaduplex and I rent out the other three units at $1000.00 per month per unit. For this property alone, I get a potential income stream of $3000.00. Now I am getting a potential income stream of $2000.00 a month from my first apartment building, $3,000.00 a month on my second building, and $3,000.00 on my third building. I have a total potential income of $8,000.00 a month. I stay in my quaduplex for another 2 years and purchase my fourth property with the money I generated from my passive income stream. This time I should have potentially accumulated $192,000.00 of passive income. I decide to only use only $25,000.00 to purchase my forth multi-family building (4th green house) as a down payment.

Now I decide to buy another quaduplex building and using only $25,000.00 for the down payment. I duplicate the same system and now my potential income stream should be very nice. I should generate $2000.00 a month from my first property, $3000.00 a month on my second property, $4,000.00 a month on my third property, and $3,000.00 a month from my fourth property. I should have a total potential income stream of $12,000.00 a month. Wow!! If $12,000.00 a month potential income does not get you excited then I do not know what will. Remember I stated earlier that I would give you a 10-year plan to build wealth in real estate. Now you are approaching your 10th year after staying in your 4th multi-family apartment for another 2 years. You should have generated $288,000.00 in two years from the four green houses that you have in your real estate portfolio. Now you are ready to buy your first commercial property (red hotel) on the tenth year.

Usually, banks like to lend you 75%-90% Loan To Value (LTV) on the commercial property. Commercial properties are a good way to start generating huge cash flow potential if you have the 10%-25% to put down on the properties. Getting the 10%-25% for the down payment is very easy. You will have to be creative when you are using this strategy. You can buy a multi-million dollar property that is generating hundreds of thousands a year by staying focused and disciplined on your ten-year plan on building wealth in real estate.

You have the power to get unlimited income by following a simple plan. People think that building wealth is hard and they are not lucky enough to be a millionaire unless they win the lottery. You have a better chance to become a self-made millionaire instead an instant millionaire from the lottery if you have the discipline, dedication, and desire. Using this strategy might not allow you to build wealth in 30 days, but you will know how to start positioning yourself towards wealth building within your first 30 days and this is extremely important when you are seeking for freedom. You can start by buying four green houses and upgrade to a red hotel.

CHAPTER 6

How to produce Intellectual Income?
You are the expert! So start getting paid...

Intellectual property is a great way to produce income by converting thoughts into dollars. Every screenplay or movie originated from somebody's mind. You can generate millions of dollars if you convert your thoughts into dollars. The main point in this chapter is that everybody has a million dollar idea. The challenge is converting the idea into dollars.

This chapter will explain how you can convert your thoughts into dollars. I believe that everyone should write a book. It is inevitable that as humans we will die. It is always good to leave something behind. One of the things that you should leave behind is a book. Whether it is an autobiography or a fictional book, print is forever. You might be long gone from this world, but your words on paper can live forever. You could also generate income from your thoughts on paper when you sell your book. You will be surprised the amount of people who want to hear what you have to say. If you take the time and do only this, you will have the capability to generate income now. I will give you an easy strategy on how you can become a published author.

This tip alone will help you generate income from writing a book. A lot of my friends and family ask me how I publish a book. I will break it down to three easy steps for you. The first thing you want to do is copyright your book. You can do this by going to www.copyrite.gov. The second step is that you will need to get is an ISBN number as well as a barcode. You can do this by going to www.barcode-us.com. The third step is finding a print on demand publisher and there are tons of companies to pick. The two companies that I recommend are www.lulu.com and www.createspace.com. I would check on their terms and conditions before you get started. Let your mind be free and place your thoughts on paper. Once you finished writing your book, you have a legitimate product that you created that can generate income. Once you have your product you will need to do some marketing. Always remember that marketing drives sales. You can generate multiple streams of income from your book. You can have an e-book, audio book, and do seminars and workshop about what you wrote. The sky is the limit.

1. You're the Expert, write the book

Everybody that has a story to tell should write a book. I am amazed to listen to many people who can talk for hours on the phone just for general purposes and never consider writing a book. I always say to myself that this person should write and promote their ideas in a book that ignites their passion. Everybody might have some knowledge in a particular subject regardless of the topic. You might surprise yourself on how much you really know on a subject.

After reading this book, I hope that I awaken a financial genius within you to write your book. As you can see, this book is very small but it is to the point. Most people feel that they must have 300 pages or more of information to be called a "book". People want to hear your thoughts and ideas. Do not be discouraged if there are 100 authors that write on that subject. You can be the 101 person that will explain the subject better. Always remember that people are always are looking for new or updated information.

Intellectual property is a good way to generate income within 30 days. In November 9, 1989, the Berlin wall of Germany fell and united the country. That was a historical moment not only for Germany, but all over the world. This year marked the birth of the Internet. We had officially made the transition from the Industrial Age to the Information Age in 1989. Information is the driving force of the world. The person who has the most information and who can get access to that information faster is a winner.

Intellectual Property is not only literature but it also refers to creations of the mind such as musical, artistic works, invention, symbols, names, images, and designs. Most people will not take the time to think. A habit that many people start to condition their mind to "laziness". People complain about their financial situation but never utilize their brainpower to figure out how they can obtain financial literacy to avoid mishaps.

This is a great strategy that you can start building residual income from your ideas. I recommend that people go to workshops and/or attend classes on how you can start putting ideas on paper. You will be surprised on how much information you can receive by going to a seminar and learning how to write a book. Anyone can do this reasonable strategy and you can start building a steady flow of income.

2. The Power of Audio Books

Some people may not find writing as a favorite activity. Personally, I hated writing while I was in school, but now all I do is write my ideas down on paper. I always enjoyed doing speaking engagements and participating in debates instead of writing. One of my favorite things that I took pleasure in was partaking in impromptu speaking contests in High School. I enjoyed having people say a topic randomly where I get 5 to 10 minute speech ready within 2 minutes. For people that have ideas but do not like to write, I suggest that you produce an audio book. This is an easy strategy to market your idea to the masses without doing a lot of writing. Many people are buying audio books and tapes from authors because their time is limited to read the information. People like to listen to authors while they are in traffic, at their desk at work, or if they want to fall asleep. Technology has made it easier for authors because now there are many authors that record their speaking engagements and upload it in a MP3 format for people to download the information online.

Depending on the value of the information, people will pay top dollar if you have a topic that people want. I have paid as much as $10,000 to attend different workshops and seminars to get information. I do not suggest people spend this much money, but I want to make a point that if you have information that people want, you can name your price. I have mentors that have audio books for sale and they are making a good living just speaking and recording their ideas. This is a great strategy on how you can start implementing in your life to start generating income.

As a businessperson I look to do something once and get unlimited income from doing that one thing. For example, I bought a piece of real estate a few years ago and I continue to receive passive income. By buying that one house, I am creating generational wealth and reinvesting my profits to get into other investments once. People should always look for strategies to do something one time and obtain a flowing stream of income to their bank accounts.

Ask yourself, "what can I write or speak about to start creating income from my ideas?" Ideas are just ideas, but finding that one idea might require additional work. I am sure that once you find your idea, you will be glad that you took the time to find it. Do not make the mistake on missing astronomical amounts of money through information. The person who has the most information will have the capabilities to produce the most money. Knowledge alone is not power, but applied knowledge will give you the most power. Record your ideas and sell them to start generating income now.

3. Seminars and Workshops

Once you write your ideas and/or record your ideas, you can produce additional income by conducting seminars and workshops. People learn by different ways and conducting a "How To" workshop will allow people to be interactive with you and ask questions. This might require some time to plan the event and get people to participate, but once you get through the preliminary part, you will see the amount of profit that you can generate by conducting seminars and workshops.

People are always willing to attend seminars and workshop. Usually the seminars and workshop might have some type of nominal fee and this is a way to start generating a flowing income stream. You can actually attend classes on how to setup a seminar and/or workshop. This is a good place to start marketing your book or audio book. You might want to consider reducing the price of your product for people who attend the seminar and/or workshop. You can get a good idea by comparing prices in your industry. Once you know what your competitors are charging you can charge slightly below their rates. If you do not have any competitors, you name your price.

If starting a workshop is not in your interest, participate as a vendor to other workshops or seminars and sell your books there. This is an effective way to market your product and build good business relationships with other entrepreneurs. You can also collaborate with different civic and religious organizations and tap into that market to help find leads. Workshops and seminars are appealing to customers. For instance, sales are a driving force towards increased income. Every person reading this book should aspire to become an entrepreneur. To be an effective entrepreneur you must have a good sales strategy to sell your products.

Information in your local library could be a helpful tool when researching topics regarding sales. Every businessperson should know how to sell or get training on sales. People often combine sales and marketing and that is a big mistake. Sales and Marketing are two different departments. Selling is the act of persuading or influencing a customer to buy (actually exchange something of value for) a product or service. Marketing is the driving force to stimulate sales. People use these interchangeably even though they are two different entities.

When you set up a workshop or conduct a seminar, you are marketing your product to increase sales. Workshops and seminars are a good way to increase your sales because you are interactive with people and people are getting hands on training on that topic. I recommend that you attend to seminars and workshops to get the maximum benefit on the subject that you are interested in, or the subject you want to generate interest in people. This is a powerful way to start generating income now. Become a student before you become a teacher. Learn from the experts that have the topic you are interested and then begin teaching others in your seminars.

CHAPTER 7

How to "produce" income online?
Getting rich in the Information Age...

Generating income online is the wave of the future. I recommend that you consider developing ways to increase your cash flow online. It is a good idea to start a website and have different affiliate marketing accounts. Before I explain a little about affiliate marketing, I want to ask a question. How many times have you seen a movie that you liked shared the movie, and recommended others watch? How many times have you tried a product that worked for you, and recommended others to try that product? People usually do this all the time. You are doing marketing for a company without reaping the benefits. Affiliate marketing is a concept that when you promote a product you will be paid.

Affiliate Marketing is a popular method of promoting web businesses in which an affiliate is rewarded for every visitor, subscriber and/or customer provided through his efforts. It is a modern variation of the practice of paying finder's fees for the introduction of new clients to a business. Compensation maybe made based on a certain value for each visit (Pay-per-click), registrant (pay-per-lead), or a commission for each customer or sale (Pay-per-sale).

The most attractive aspect of affiliate marketing, from the merchant's viewpoint, is that no payment is due to an affiliate until results arise. Some e-commerce sites, such as www.amazon.com run their own affiliate programs while other e-commerce vendors use third party service provided by intermediaries like www.commissionjunction.com, and www.linkshare.com to track traffic or sales referred from affiliates. Some businesses owe much of their growth and success to this marketing technique. I cannot emphasize enough the importance of marketing and its benefits on driving sales.

All well known and established companies, such as Wal-Mart, Target, Office Depot, and Best Buy have affiliate programs on their websites. You just have to go to their websites and scroll to the bottom and click on "affiliates" or "affiliate program" to sign up free. I recommend that you go to www.melvintalks.com to get more information on affiliate marketing and other ways you can make money online.

1. E-bay is paving the way

EBay is a great place to start a home-based business to help generate additional income. Many people are looking for alternative ways to generate wealth. Some people want to have a business and do not know where to start. This strategy has created fortunes for many people around the world by simply taking pictures and posting it online. Ecommerce is truly paving the way people are doing business in the future. I recommend that people establish an eBay account regardless if they use this strategy. You can find many items at a discounted price from thousands of different vendors who are looking for your business.

EBay is the biggest online marketplace in the world with millions of products sold . Potential buyers log on every day to buy specific products or see what is available. An online eBay business is very simple to establish and will not take long for you start up. You might ask the question, "How can I get the products to sell?" You can start by finding gently used clothes, toys, kitchenware, tools, and different accessories that you might have in your home that you barely use now. You will be surprised what people are willing to buy on eBay. Remember, your trash is somebody's treasure.

The first thing to do if you are interested in having an eBay business is to open an eBay account. This is free to do and will only take a few minutes. You should choose the eBay site for the country that you live in, but note that you can use your eBay ID to buy or sell things on any of the other country sites once you start your account.

I will also give you another tip that you can go to your local flea market, find items for a very reasonable price, and resell that item on eBay. You can start making money without using your own money by finding items and using a little creativity. In the past, I have purchased real estate, businesses, and other investments without using my money. It might take OPM (Other People Money) to fund my deals, but I will not have to worry about using my personal cash to find great investment opportunities.

2. Benefit without setting up a website

Having a website is a valuable way to increase income for your business. Due to the rapid speed of technology, people are able to view your products or services instantly by viewing your website. Having a professional website can cost a few hundred or thousands of dollars. Why spend money developing a website when you can market your products for free?

If you want to start an eBay business, you do not have to spend any time building your own website or trying to get people to visit your new website. You do not have to worry about the traffic, as eBay provides this for you, with millions of people all over the world logging in every day. This is a great way to generate income within 30 days because you do not need out of pocket expenses.

Many people are only satisfied with having a full-time job, but I recommend that people have a part-time business along with a full time job. Many people with full-time jobs also look for another part-time or full-time job to earn extra income to cover their expenses. There are many opportunities in developing other streams of income without sacrificing your time in a part-time job.

The second best asset that everyone has in life is his or her time. I remember growing up and attending grade school, my teachers will always tell me to use my time wisely. I never understood why they told me this every time when I was doing something that was not suppose to. People spend a lot of time with their employers, their civic organizations, their family and friends, and they never invest time to start a part-time business. I hope that you will gain valuable information to help supplement your income if you have a full-time job. The best asset that everyone has is the mind. Unfortunately, you cannot take your brain, set it on the table of a loan officer at the bank and say, "Add this to my list of assets!" Your mind is the most powerful asset regardless of your present situation. Invest in your financial education and the money and other assets will start to develop.

The benefit to have a business and market your product where millions of people are constantly viewing is priceless. Everybody has an entrepreneur spirit inside them that is waiting to emerge and develop huge profits and dividends. Just use your imagination or use some of the strategies that I recommend to start generating income in 30 days.

Once you establish that you are in business you just wait for the bidders to come your way. You can sell specific items or many different items. I recommend that you start selling things that you have and look for similar items to see if you have any competition to match the price.

As an experienced user of E-bay, I have purchased books from E-bay and resold the book online after I finished reading the information. For example, I bought a gently used book for $15.00 and sold the same book after I finished reading it for $25.00. This is a prime example how I generated income in less than 30 days. Before you consider a yard sale, set up an eBay account and see if you can maximize your profits by exposing your product to millions of people around the world.

Just imagine that you can make an additional $150.00 for selling items that you rarely use. If you do not think that $150.00 is a lot of money, give it to me. It would be an honor to get that cash from you any day. Any income that you receive that does not require a lot of work is a good thing. I get excited when I find $1.00 on the ground that nobody claims. I remember finding $20.00 in my jacket that I did not know was there. That $20.00 made me so happy that it turned a bad day to a GREAT one. Do not worry about the dollar amount; rather worry about the process and the habit of generating income. Do not get discouraged when you are receiving only small increments of cash that is flowing into your pocket. Be consistent and those small checks will add up.

I was once in a network marketing company, and I remember when I received my first check. My first few checks were only $25.00, but I was so excited that I received a check that I started showing people the checks that I was receiving. Over time, I was getting $1,000.00 and different dollar amounts by staying positive and consistent. This might sound strange, but showing people my checks helped me recruit more people. I recruited more people in my organization by showing them my smaller checks compared to just talking to random people about the product. People saw the excitement in my eyes and people knew that I was building a business and having fun at the same time.

I am sure you are all familiar with the TV show "Who wants to be a Millionaire?" and I replied, "I would not mind being a 'Thousandaire'!" I will take any income that put extra money in my pocket regardless of the amount. Concentrate on developing strategies that will help generate additional income and the amount of money will keep multiplying. Focus on developing a part-time business if you have a full-time job. It is your employer's job to give you your paycheck and it is your job to invest your money and/or find a business by using your paychecks. Many people live from paycheck to paycheck instead of setting aside money for a business. On the contrary, if you are putting funds away, I must offer congratulations on your continuance in this disciplined process. If you are not putting away money, you should start doing it now. Start putting away at least 10% of your income and use it on qualified investments. Money will arrive in increasing quantities to anyone who puts aside at least 10% to create an estate for their future and family.

3. Potential Income

The potential income that you can generate online is endless. The more effort you put into your online business the more income you can generate. Practice selling something online and see if it can sell within 30 days. I challenge every reader to start an online business and be paid within 30 days; hopefully, you will be paid sooner! You can also get creative on the Internet by having your own affiliate business. This is a practice in which a business rewards one or more affiliates for each visitor or customer brought about by the affiliate's marketing efforts. You can go to www.google.com and get tremendous amount of information on how to participate in this booming Internet Marketing wave. I know a few people who generated tremendous amounts of money by having their own Internet Optimization Company or Search Engine Optimization (SEO). This is the process of improving the volume or quality of traffic to a website.

You can explore all of the possibilities by having your own company that can provide this service once you understand the concepts and procedures to do this. You can find out more about Internet Marketing, e-mail marketing, interactive advertising, social media optimization, and web analytics all online and you can start your own business almost overnight once you understand what you are doing.

You can also start a pay-per-click business as well. This is a very lucrative business and I have seen and heard many people build an Internet empire by this strategy. I know that this is a great way to get started. I believe you can find tremendous amount of information on Google and other websites and you can get started today. It is easy to do but you have to know the rules in order to play the game effectively. Pay per click (PPC) is an Internet advertising model used on search engines, advertising networks, and content websites, such as blogs, where advertisers only pay when a user actually clicks on an advertisement to visit the advertisers' website. You might get a few pennies, but they add up to dollars fast if you have the proper setups. Billions of people browse through the Internet almost every day and if you drive over a million people from Internet traffic those pennies will add up real fast.

CHAPTER 8

How to produce income by trading?
Generating income regardless of the market trend...

1. What are Stock Options?

The stock market has many terms and jargon that might seem very confusing. Once you understand the language, you will understand how to play the game. The stock market is like Las Vegas for the rich. You can make a lot of money or you lose a lot of money depending on your experience and strategies that you use. I will simplify some of the language so that the beginner investor will understand how to participate in the stock market and profit regardless of the status of the stock market.

I will use one example that I will cross-reference with all three topics in this book. I will also consider having an online broker that has the ability of virtual trading. Virtual trading is a great way to learn without using your money. Once you become comfortable in trading stock options or writing covered calls, you can fund your account and put your money to work.

Investing in the stock market can be very risky, but you minimize your risk through financial education. Acquiring more financial education will result in less exposure to risks. The stock market is also risky for people who know what they are doing. The stock market can be either predicable or unpredictable depending on the situation. I research and study graphs, charts, reviews, and cross-reference information before I get into any deal in the stock market.

The stock market is truly a money making machine once you understand the rules, terminology, and the risks that are involved. I do not recommend that anyone try these strategies unless they are experienced and or received additional information from people that are skilled in this field. As always, please consult with your stockbroker, financial advisor, or legal professional to see if this strategy will work for you.

Stock options are financial instruments that convey the right, but not the OBLIGATION, to engage in a future transaction on a security. In other words, the person buying does not have to exercise this right to buy. I will give a great example so you can visualize this concept. This can be complicated to understand but I am sure that the example that I will provide will help clear any vague ideas that you may have regarding to stock options. I recommend that you consult with your stockbroker to see if your current stocks are optional. This way you can add this strategy to your portfolio.

What is the Rule of 72?

Many investors use the rule of 72 to determine the amount of time it will take double their money from their initial investment. Many investors and bankers use this hypothetical formula as a guide to determine the length of time to receive profits. You simply take the constant interest rate and divide that by the number 72 and you will get the amount of time your investment will take to double in value.

For example, if you invest $100.00 in a savings account in your local bank with a yield of 3% interest per year. You can determine how long it will take your investment to double in value by using this formula. You divide 3 by 72 and you will get 24. If you put $100.00 in your account today, you will have $200.00 in 24 years.

Most people will have investments in mutual funds, money markets, Thrift Savings Plan, or 401(k) investment accounts. Usually, you might receive on an average of 12% interest per year. However, due to drastic changes in the stock market and increased fund management fees you might receive less than this conservative amount. For illustrative purposes only, I will keep a constant rate of return of 12% per year. You divide 12 by 72 and you will get 6. Keeping your money in these investment vehicles, your initial investment will take 6 years to double in value.

Investing in Mutual Funds and Company provided retirement accounts might seem very exciting compared to leaving your funds in a savings account. People usually have their funds in either one or both of these investment vehicles. Most people will not take the time to invest in their financial education and use different financial strategies. Personally, I prefer to invest in stock options. I receive an average of 24% interest per month. However, I do receive higher rates of return but for illustrative purposes, I will keep the constant the same at 24% interest. You divide 24 by 72 you will get 3. By keeping my money in the stock market using this strategy my money will double in value every 3 months.

Investing in Stock Options is an aggressive way to build wealth in the stock market. You are not getting just 24% ROI (Return On Investment), you are receiving profits by orders of magnitude. It is quite possible to receive up to 1,000% interest per month from your initial investment by utilizing this technique in the stock market.

Get a broker or a financial advisor that will give you more details on how to start investing in stock options and writing covered calls. Remember the person who has and can process information faster will be successful in this Information Age. Investing in stock options is a good alternative way to help protect your money and minimize your risks. All investments are risky; however, you have the power to minimize your risk through financial education.

The Example that will give you a practical understanding of Options:

You have a house for sale for $200,000.00 and you want to move into another neighborhood. You decided that moving will be the best for you and your family. You decide to sell the house because you want to move to an area where the school district for your children meets your approval. You had your house in the market for 12 months and nobody is interested in your property so you begin to get frustrated because the time that your house has been in the market is making you anxious.

I do my research in your area and I notice that there are some future developments in that city. I notice in my research that your house has been in the market for a while so I decided to invest in your neighborhood. In my findings, I see that your house has been on the market for a while and you might be motivated to sell your property.

I knock on your door and tell you that I am interested in buying your property and I want to know the sales price. You tell me that you want to sell the house for $200,000.00 but you are willing to negotiate the price. I tell you instead that I will only buy your house under certain conditions. I have piqued your interest and you are now listening to my terms.

In my proposal, I decide to give you $10,000.00 if you give me at least 30 days to decide to buy your property. Within my 30-day period, I have the option to buy or walk away from your property. I inform you that you can keep my $10,000.00 regardless if I buy the house in 30 days. However, our agreement indicates that I am the exclusive buyer until my 30-day option has lapsed. You are excited because you will be paid regardless of the outcome of my decision. We sign the contract and we are in a full agreement.

A few days later, a major developer, let us say Wal-Mart is buying out everyone in the neighborhood to build a supercenter and a parking lot. Wal-Mart is offering homeowners one million dollars to every homeowner in the neighborhood for this major development in your area. You are very excited because if I do not buy this property. Wal-Mart will surely buy this house from you.

After you realized that Wal-Mart is offering you a million dollars, you tell Wal-Mart that you can not sell your property because you are under contract. Wal-Mart informs you that they need your property and ask for my information. You give them my information and Wal-Mart contacts me.

Wal-Mart informs me that they want the property and is willing to offer me one million dollars. I am happy to sell the property to Wal-Mart because I am about to be paid. I tell Wal-Mart to cut a check to you for $200,000.00 and cut me a check for $800,000.00 and Wal-Mart will have ownership of your property.

You are happy that you sold your property and you received the full amount of your asking price. I am happy that my $10,000.00 option did not expire and I made $800,000.00 from my initial investment. Wal-Mart is happy because they have the real estate to develop the shopping center to support the community. This is a win-win deal by all parties involved. This is how it will look like when we all live in a perfect world.

The three parties involved in the transaction is a perfect example of the strategies that are in this book. You are the person using the (**covered call**) technique. You are receiving a monthly check to sell your stock at a predetermined price. I am the person using a (**straight option**) technique. I am putting a substantial lower amount to control a block of stock. Wal-Mart is a good example if you are called out of your stock position in the (**options game**) in the stock market. You profit in a covered call position by receiving income by me and income when you sell your house. In other words, you have the opportunity to be paid twice using a covered call strategy. I can reap enormous profit by trading options because any small movement in the stock market will result in a magnified movement in the option market.

I gave this example for illustration purposes only and for clarification on how using options as an additional stream of portfolio income can work for you. You might have to read this section a few times to grasp this technique. Check with your stockbroker to find out if you have optional stocks. I personally use OptionsXpress online brokers to conduct my transactions. To set up an account is very easy just go to www.optionxpress.com, www.tradeking.com, www.sharebuilder.com just to name a few. Check out these websites for more details. There are other online brokers, just shop around and find the one that fits your style of trading.

Opening an online brokerage account will open the doors and doing paper trades will increase your intelligence on technical investing. You also have the capabilities to practice by using paper money before putting your personal money to work. Once you master how to trade options, it does not matter how the stock market performs, because you will make more money. Reinvest your earnings until you have an Army of Money working for you and you are the commander in Chief watching it all happen before your eyes.

Learn the terminologies from Bull Put Spreads, Calandar Spreads, Strattles, strangles, and take advantage of the stock market without any worries about the direction that it is going. This type of technical investing alone will help you generate income almost instantly if you apply the knowledge that you learned. People pay thousands of dollars just to get training on this type of training.

I have personal financial advisors that help me with my stock option trading; you should look to find a coach who is a master option trader and learn from them. Compare prices from different companies by simply goggling search stock option coaches. You can find endless of opportunities on the Internet and it is just a click away. This book is just a guide that introduces alternative ways to generate income. Always remember that all great person and athletes have coaches.

You must have the desire to do your research and check it out for yourself. I encourage all my readers to investigate all of these strategies and you will see it is possible to generate income in 30 days or maybe sooner if you master one or some of the recommendations in this book.

2. Writing Covered Calls

Writing a covered call is a technical strategy that allows you to make large sums of money in the stock market. Online trading is my second favorite strategy next to real estate. You can make a good steady flow of income by just this strategy alone in the stock market. What I am revealing in this section of the book is worth more than the price you have paid for this book. I have made thousands of dollars by using this strategy and trading straight options in this book. I recommend that you do this strategy in a bull or an upward trend market. You can generate monthly cash flow from the stocks that you already own. When selling a call option, you are contracting the delivery of the stock you own at a price (strike price) for a specific amount of time (option month). In other words, the buyer has the right to buy your stock but is not obligated.

If you are in a covered call position, it doesn't matter if you get called out of your position. Your intention should be generating cash flow from your stock by renting it out. Being called out from your option position is a bonus to you. You can generate money every month until you get called out from your position. When you get called out of your position, you will be paid for the purchase price that was predetermined by the market.

I recommend that you continue to reinvest your profits and seek additional streams of income because this allows your investments to multiply like compound interest. I am sure if you search the word "covered call" in the Internet search engine, you will find volumes of information on this strategy. I recommend that you practice by opening a virtual account and learn by using virtual money online. Options and Covered Calls can be risky investments because options usually expire on the third Friday of every month.

Once you understand the rules and the terminologies of Options, this will be a great way to generate income within 30 days or possibly less. Always consult with your stockbrokers and financial advisors to get more information on this wonderful strategy to build unlimited income in the stock market.

3. Trading Straight Options

Straight Option Trading is my favorite technical strategy in the stock market. I am constantly researching and finding Options on stocks and wait for profits. Through my extensive research on chart reading, graphs, historical data, and other indicators, I manage my risks when I invest in the Option Market.

Some of the basic terminologies that you must be familiar with is a contract. A contract consists of 100 option shares. This includes both covered calls and straight options. I would recommend to writing covered calls on stocks that range from $5.00-$25.00 per share. Options are usually a lot cheaper than the actual stock. You have the opportunity to control a $100.00 per share stock for $5.00 or even less.

When there is a small movement of the price of the stock in the market, a magnified movement will occur in the option market. Depending on the direction of the stock market, I will determine if I need to buy a 'call' option or a 'put' option. I know this might seem a little confusing, but they are just opposite from each other. I always say, "CALL up and PUT down"

You buy call options when you think the stock is going to go up in a bullish trend. You buy put options when you think the stock market is going down in a bearish trend.

Practice looking at charts and other indicators to determine whether you should buy a call or a put option. A call options provides the right to buy a specific number of shares of a security at a set price. The set price is called a strike price in the option market. A put option provides the right to sell. You or the option holder has the choice or the option holder have the choice to exercise the option before the expiration date. Usually the expiration is on the Third Friday of every month. The person who sold the option must fulfill the commitment on the contract as soon as the person is called out.

This strategy might be a little difficult to understand, but invest in your education and learn this strategy. I personally invested my time to learn this strategy for a couple of years before putting my money on the line. After I have put in the time to learn this strategy, I would receive monthly income by investing in the option market. Again, options are very risky because they expire. Trading stock options is a good way to protect from further losses in the stocks that you currently own. This strategy can give you income on a monthly or daily basis. The greater the risks means the greater the reward. Control your risks by trading options in the stock market.

CHAPTER 9

How to produce income in Network Marketing?
The upside down pyramid...

1. Why Network Marketing?

Network Marketing is a business distribution model that allows a parent company to market its products directly to consumers by means of relationship referrals and sales. I learned many valuable skills from different network marketing companies that I still use in my daily life. Network marketing has different products for sale, but focus on the training and support system and not the product.

Network Marketing is a good way to start generating income to help with your financial situation. I know many people who participate in network marketing and they are making money hand over fists by this strategy to build wealth. MLM is a good way to have a business with a low overhead and startup costs. You can make huge profits with a start up fee for most companies under $500.00. You will have a business for yourself with the support you need to start accumulating wealth.

You will call yourself an Independent distributor, associate, or a consultant. You might even have an extravagant title but your primary duties are to sell a product or service to the masses and you will receive a steady stream of residual income or commissions. You will represent the parent company and awarded a commission based upon the volume of product sold through your business organizations that you brought into the business.

It helps when you are passionate about the product and personally seen results from using it. People are always making referrals or recommendations, so why not get paid for making a recommendation to try a product? Your testimony alone can help sell the product. If you saw a movie last night and thought it was a good movie, you might recommend that movie for me to watch, but you will never receive credit for making that referral. This concept is the same in network marketing. You are recommending a product or service and telling people why they should benefit from it as well. Always consider the product and support system before you decide to join a MLM company.

2. Endless Residual Income

Once you become passionate about a product or service, you will not have to worry about selling to people. You will generate sales from your excitement and your testimony alone. You can start generating great income if you like to give referrals or testimonies. Always consider the product and the ways in which it can help people. When joining a MLM company, you will be a distributor to get the product wholesale. You will then earn a commission based on the sales efforts of your organization that you bring into the business and/or on the products that you directly sale. The people that you bring into the business are usually called a downline of independent distributors and you get a percentage of their profits on their sales. Your downline also built a customer base, thereby expanding the overall organization. Additionally, distributors can earn a profit by retailing products they purchased from the parent company.

You can receive endless amount of money from people you do not even know or the person that you brought into the business do not know but you are still being paid. Many people might get confused and start calling this a pyramid scheme. This is not the case in network marketing; this is like a triangle upside down. You want to help as many people as possible so the money will funnel down to you. A true pyramid or (triangle) is the structure of other companies. You will have the CEO or Director that will get majority of the money and everybody else will be paid a smaller cut. So one person is at the top and everybody else is at the bottom.

MLM encourages you to bring more people to the business, put them on top, and help them with their business. This is how a funnel will look like when you join a network marketing company. The more people are paid the more you will get paid. You will benefit from the people that you brought into the business your (downline) from their sales efforts as well as your own. This arrangement is similar to franchise arrangements where royalties are paid from the sales of individual franchise operations to the franchisor.

Every MLM company might have different compensation packages and I recommend that you research and find the company that will have the best product/service, support system, and compensation plan along with a low initial investment fee. There can be multiple levels of people receiving royalties from one person's sales or performance. Make sure that you do your due diligence because there are also companies out there that rip you off and under investigation. Consult with appropriate personnel to see if this source of alternative income is right for you.

3. Get the EDUCATION

I recommend that people join a MLM company to gain skills that will help you in personal development. I joined MLM companies because I know that they have good trainings and meetings that I need for personal development. You can find so many companies that are in different industries. There are health and wellness companies, Travel, Communications, and much more. Many companies are turning to a MLM systems increase sales. Many people do not like to feel like that they have been "sold" up a sales transaction, instead people want to feel like they are in control.

You will learn how to sell by listening to the consumer and let the product sell itself. I also recommend that you pick a MLM company so you can attend to their seminars and to network. The education that you will receive from a good MLM company is priceless. I have joined over five different MLM companies and I have learned valuable lessons from all of them.

A true investor will invest in their education. By you purchasing this book, you are taking the first step to your financial education. This book is exposing the multiple ways to start generating income right now. You are now able to research and learn how you can start applying some of these strategies in your life.

Please refer to my step-by-step manuals on each topic to get additional information on the stream of income or learn from other experts that will help guide you in your financial endeavors. Start applying this information and start reaping the benefits now. I always invest in financial educational development products to get a cutting edge in life. Someone told me a saying that always sticks to my head every day,

"When you're green you grow, when you're ripe you rot." This statement constantly reminds me that I don't want to stop learning because I do not want to "rot" by living on old ideas and old information that will not help me today.

Get additional information on how you can start getting alternative ways to earn extra money besides only getting a paycheck from a full-time job and earning a paycheck from your employer. It is your employer's job to make sure you get a paycheck, but it is your job to decide what you will do with that paycheck. I recommend that you invest in your education and start learning how you can generate income now.

MLM is a good place to start to build a legitimate business with little or no money out of your pocket. Your ROI (Return On Investment) is infinite if you join the right company, at the right place, at the right time. Timing is everything when you consider joining a MLM company because this might affect your success. Choose a MLM that will give you the best training you will need to take you to the next level. Always consult with your financial and legal advisor to determine if the company is right for you.

CHAPTER 10

How can I transform into a Cash flow Producer?
The more you produce the more you will get paid...

How can I transform into a producer?

This chapter will help with the transition from being a consumer to a producer. Everything is created in the mind; the problem is making it into reality. Many people that are faced with challenges and obstacles that prevent them from achieving their goals. Building wealth is a consistent plan that you must apply daily. This book is designed to open your mind to give you additional ways you can turn your trash into cash.

Many people want to be wealthy, but few people are willing to pay the price to be consistent and remain disciplined throughout this journey. Every day I have the power to choose and I choose to be a producer and a rich person. I often learn from my disappointments and mistakes, but I continue to strive towards financial freedom. I know if I am unsuccessful, I can always take the easy way out and seek security.

People are imprisoned in their mind and can not visualize being financially free. The key to your financial freedom relies on you and you alone. It is so easy to remain complacent and never seek out new ideas and a new approach towards financial freedom. It is common for people to remain at their job for many years and working everyday living from paycheck to paycheck because this is a safe secure way to survive.

Due to the fast pace of information, having only one stream of income will widen the gap from your true financial prosperity that you deserve. Everyone reading this book has the potential to try some of these strategies and start generating income now. Some of these strategies will take additional research. Wealth is measured in time and not in money. The true meaning of wealth is the amount of time that you can survive without working. My mother always told me that if you want to understand something, you give an example or a "for instance" of what you learned. For instance, if your total expenses every month are $3,000.00 and your have $6,000.00 in the bank, your wealth is only two months. You will be able to pay all of your total expenses without changing your lifestyle and you should survive for a couple of months until you generate more income or you lower your expenses.

The challenge that many people have is limited cash reserves in the bank. If you only have one stream of income, you will be in financial trouble. Having multiple streams of income is critical and the way to build and maintain wealth. You could start generating wealth today by having three piggy banks and actively placing funds in the bank everyday. The labels on your piggy banks should be saving, investing, and charity. You should make the habit everyday by placing money in these banks. To become a producer lies not in dollar amount but rather in habit.

You will become financially free because you are actively changing the way you think and the importance of achieving financial freedom. Once you start developing the habit of actively putting funds in your three piggy banks, don't rob the bank!!!

People are always tempted to rob their earnings without their earnings finding profitable employment to multiply. Your money is eager to multiply if given the chance. I personally recommend that you place at least 10% of your gross earnings in each bank and do not force it into impossible earnings or utilize on romantic desires and investments. The savings bank should be funds to keep ensuring security in case your stream of income runs low or if you lose your job. The money in this bank should cover your expenses for at least 6 months. If your total expenses are $2,000.00 a month, you should have at least $12,000.00 in this bank.

The investing bank should be funds used to buy profitable investments and to create multiple streams of income. You can use the money that you generated to help with down payment assistance for your investments. Usually, you can find good investments without using your money. I highly recommend using (OPM), Other Peoples' Money, to purchase assets that will generate and create wealth. You can generate some of the strategies by using OPM requiring little to no money.

I always believe that the more you give the more you receive. Whether you give your time and/or money, you will be rewarded from your cheerful giving. This third bank should have money to help charities, churches, or any other civic organizations that support the programs of your choice. You should always have a philanthropic arm towards giving.
The transformation to become a producer gets easier if you are actively doing things, and if you think like a wealthy person. These banks will force you to actively participate in your financial learning and will assist in remaining focused and disciplined towards financial freedom. Building wealth

is a simple formula that will require a lot of discipline. Many financial advisors might recommend you live below your means when faced with adversity. They will tell you to cut up your credit cards, eliminate all of your debt, live miserable for the rest of your lives, and deprive yourself from many desires. This is good advice for some, but I find that many wealthy people do not follow this advice.

Everyone's circumstances are different and it is always good to get different advisors and cater them to your needs. If you find yourself getting financial advice from your broke neighbor, then you might need to seek professionals who are skilled in the field of investing. Seeking advice from those who are not professionals in the field is a disaster waiting to happen. It is like going to an auto mechanic and asking them to give you expert advice in gourmet cooking. There might be a strong possibility that the auto mechanic does not know anything about gourmet cooking, but the mechanic might not be an expert because he spends most of his time fixing automobiles.

Be very careful where you get your financial advice and seek professionals who are skilled in the area of investing. I would also watch out for handling your money to different investment vehicles without you knowing all the facts about the vehicles. I have mentioned some interesting ways where you can start generating income, but it is ultimately up to you to do your due diligence and get all of the facts on the subject.

The Internet is a great place to find everything you need on different subjects. The Internet allowed people to think outside of the box and open their mind to variety of interesting facts on any subject imaginable. With this powerful tool, you can obtain unlimited amount income by creating an idea and developing it into cash. I have mentioned several times in this book that money is just an idea and ideas are everywhere and everybody has them.

You have the power to generate income and create income out of thin air. Everybody has this power and everybody has the potential to become extremely wealthy. The sad truth about this is that many people will not put their creative information to work. They are prepared to remain safe and secure with their jobs and watch life pass by them financially. There are three types of people. The first type makes things happen. The second type watches what happens. The third type wondered what happened. Which one are you?

Regardless of the volatile economy, your business should thrive financially because you invested in a recession proof business. Not all businesses will survive during a downward spiral trend in the economy; recession proof businesses will not only survive but also surpass the company expectations. I can list hundreds of businesses that are recession proof, but for illustrative purposes, I will only mention just a few. Always remember that through the power of the Internet you will find many opportunities that are considered "recession proof" it is just a 'click' away. Many people love to start a business that will fulfill their passions and dreams and make an endless amount of money. However, your dreams and thoughts might be suited for only you. When you consider starting a business, you want to cater to the masses. Once you identify how your business can help more and more people, you will receive endless amount of income to fulfill your personal dreams and desires. It might be easier to purchase a pre-existing business that is already receiving positive cash flow. Cash flow is the blood that runs through a business veins. Always remember to review the business cash flow before you consider the investment.

Do not be embarrassed by asking questions if the numbers do not look right. Review the financial statements because they always tell the story on the business.

In addition, I recommended that you have a CPA to help go over the numbers on the business. Depending on the business, it might look good on paper but really, it is struggling financially. Always get a professional to help you go over the numbers just in case the numbers are skewed. You can find a CPA anywhere in your local phone book or on the Internet. Find a CPA that fits your personality and who you feel comfortable with to share your personal financial information. I wish I knew the right CPA for you but only you will know who will best fit your needs.

Suggestions

Recycling is a good way to preserve and protect the environment. People are always recommending consumers to recycle. I remember living in New York going around and collecting aluminum soda cans from the street when I was a kid. I have always had an entrepreneur spirit and I noticed that I would get $.05 per can. This might not seem much but I saw $500.00 instead of $.05. I would collect the cans and exchange cans for cash at the local grocery store. I do not remember the name of the store but they will give me a voucher and I would give it to the cashier for cash. This was my first lesson on how trash flow can turn into cash flow.

I would go around town with a large trash bags and collect cans that was left on the ground. I would do this after school and on weekends. Instead of playing with my friends and getting into trouble, I decided that I would do this so I can have money to put in my piggy bank. I made my $500.00 that I saw mentally with additional money to spend on games and other toys from cans that people simply threw away. This is a perfect example of how you can generate income within 30 days. People are beginning to recognize that recycling can reap huge dividends. Locating the trash to sell is so easy and usually you can get these items free. Many people do not realize that people would pay for junk cars sitting in your yard. Currently, there are people and companies that offer a nice amount for your junk car. The reason that they are offering you cash for your car is because of the metal will be sold to recycle plants for a fee.

I would consider researching how you can start generating income from recycling. Through the power of the Internet, you can learn how to start a company and gather up trash for cash. Instead of throwing or giving away your trash, do research to see if you get compensated for it. I am not recommending that you spend your day looking for trash or aluminum cans as I did when I was a kid; however, find opportunities available out there for you can generate extra cash.

Every day when I drive on the interstate, I see pieces of tires that lay on the side of the road or on the road. After researching tires and their alternative uses, you can get income by collecting old tires and selling them. Scrap tires are commonly used for Tire-Derived Fuel. To name some of major combustion facilities that use Tire-Derived Fuel are cement kilns, power plants and pulp/paper boilers.

This book is for informational and educational purposes only. I recommend how you might be able to tap into this industry and see how you can profit from selling trash. A company named **teracycle** will pay you for giving them recycled products. They will pay you $.25 for cell phones, and $0.02 for drink pouches, cookie wrappers, potato chips bags, cereal boxes, you name it. If you got trash, you get paid… Check out teracycle.net to get more information about the company and their mission.

Always ask yourself how you can generate income, do not stump your brain by stating that you cannot generate income. This is a primary example that income is all around us; all we have to do is find it. You can find your income on the side of the road, in your house, or in the trash. People make huge profits for selling antiques, rare coins, trading cards, and comic books. Income is everywhere and this book will open your mind so that you can start generating income within 30 days. There is a saying that goes, *"Excuses build bridges to nowhere, and monuments of nothing. Those who practice them seldom accomplish anything at all."* This was a powerful quote that I heard over the years and always stick in the back of my mind. Stop making excuses and start taking action on building wealth and generating unlimited income.

The SWOT Theory

Strengths, Weakness, Opportunities and Threats theory is credited to **Albert Humphrey**, who led a research project at Stanford University in the 1960s and 1970s using data from Fortune 500 companies. SWOT analysis is a strategic method used to evaluate the strengths, weakness, opportunities, and threat in a business venture or any project that you might be interested.

STRENGTHS   OPPORTUNITIES

WEAKNESS   THREATS

This is a great concept when you are analyzing any deal. Always do your due diligence in any venture to know the strengths, weakness, opportunities, and threats. Do not get excited on the concept without first evaluating the situation. Do not focus on the strengths and forget about the other aspects of the SWOT theory. Mastering this concept alone can make you millions if you have a team of people to help you in your SWOT analysis.

Many people believe that going to school and getting a good job with great benefits is the formula for success. New entrepreneurs are institutionalized from being an employee that given any little resistance will run back to being a secure employee, rather than instead of moving forward towards freedom. One of my favorite movies of all time is the Matrix. If you have not seen this movie, you will see many hidden subliminal messages throughout the movie on the importance on financial literacy. One of my favorite parts of the movie is when Mr. Anderson had to choose either the red or the blue pill. The beginning steps of his destiny depended on the color he chose. I encourage everybody reading the book to watch the Matrix and find the hidden messages that applies to finances. You might have missed the messages from all of the action and martial arts in the movie. Listen closely to the words of the characters and I assure you that the meaning behind the words is extremely powerful towards financial freedom.

In a nutshell, this movie is about a computer Hacker named Thomas A. Anderson also known as NEO. It is very interesting that the word 'NEO' is an anagram of the word of 'ONE'. NEO is also Greek for 'NEW', suggesting messianic overtones for his mission in the Matrix. Neo lives in the world of the 'Matrix', an illusory construct in which humans are connected to a massive computer system that simulates the world of the late 20th century. This system was developed by intelligent machines to keep the human population as tools for the machines' survival; the machines use a form of fusion in addition to the bioelectrical energy of human beings as their primary energy source. The machines had relied upon solar power, but after the war between humans and machines broke out, humans cut off the machines' energy source by creating an immense cloud of nanomachines that blocked out the sunlight. Those who live their 'ENTIRE LIVES' connected to the Matrix are unaware that their reality is not in fact 'REAL', nor that there is a human rebellion by the few 'FREE' humans in the city of Zion. Zion is the last human city on the plant Earth after a cataclysmic nuclear war between humankind and sentient Machines. NEO is believed to be the 'ONE' to help end the war between machines and humans.

If you still believe that going to school to get a good job and living paycheck to paycheck is your reality, then you might have to ask yourself 'Am I still in the Matrix?' I am not discrediting people who are employees, living paycheck to paycheck, but there is another reality, and that is freedom. Do not be a slave that is giving your employer all of your energy and time. Instead of falling for the trap of working overtime to make your employer rich, work on building your business on your time from portions of your paycheck. The rich do not work for money; they have their money work for them. I am not suggesting that you quit your job and start building a business. There are certain things that I would recommend that you do before you leave your job. You want the power that if you decide to work as an employee it is because you choose to and not because you must in order to survive. It is your employer's job to ensure that you get your paycheck, but it is your job to make yourself rich. You have the choice of taking the red or blue pill, or to be financial secure or financial free. If you choose to be wealthy, it is a simple process, just stay disciplined and know the rules. Everybody has the power to be rich just change your mind and you will see that we live in a world in abundance of wealth to go around. The ultimate question that you need to ask your self is, "Am I the ONE?" You have the power to get out of the matrix and get into your road to financial freedom. Once you identify your financial problem the question you need to ask yourself is HOW am I going to get out the financial rut?

I mentioned earlier that words are powerful, so be careful on how you use them in a sentence. Many people are enslaved in their mind and do not realize that they are in prison. This sole purpose of this book is to expand your reality. I have mentioned a few strategies and recommended books to read that will assist in your journey towards freedom. There are so much more information on wealth building that can be easily accessible if you expand your reality. Generating income is a simple process but it is not so easy without discipline. Think of ways how you can help the masses, and the masses of cash will start coming towards you. The more people you help the more you can earn. Start creating your wealth within next 30 days!

Melvin's Words of Wisdom and final thought

"The More Wisdom you know the more you can earn!"
-M. Peterson-

Thank you for taking the time to read this book. I want to leave you with a final thought. These are only a few ideas of many to help give you a jump-start on wealth building and generating income. I encourage for you to begin establishing your goals in life and what you plan to accomplish. Without a written plan on where you are going, you are just going around in a circle like a dog chasing his tail or the proper term "stuck in the 'Rat Race'".

I recommend for everyone who wants to start generating income to start asking questions and keep an open mind to the endless possibilities on wealth creation. We are in the Information Age and access to information is at the palm of our hands. I would go to the Internet search engine and ask questions on building wealth or anything that you want to learn. I would find out who is Carlos Slim? What is the Federal Reserve? How to trade FOREX? What are stock Options? The questions should go on and on.

I recommend that everyone put at least 10% of their income towards saving, investing, and giving back to different charitable organizations. It is never the dollar amount; it is the habit that will change your situation. Health and wealth are like daily practices and a way of life that runs parallel. If you want to be healthy, you have to take the necessary steps, remain disciplined, change your lifestyle, and develop good eating habits. The same applies to building wealth. I would surround myself with people who have similar goals or achieved goals that you might have. A friend of mine once told me that you can go fast alone, but you want to go fast and far with a team! Whether you want to start an organic business, a franchise, or just want to be an employee, you have the possibilities to do it by investing in yourself and constantly asking yourself "HOW CAN I MAKE MY DREAMS COME TRUE?"

To get more information on events, future books, and other products, please visit my website at www.melvintalks. com. Thank you for your interest and make sure to listen Blackanomics on channel 169 The Power on XM satellite radio to get updated information on the financial markets and additional strategies on wealth creation. Always remember that the trend is your friend and you want to position yourself in front of the opportunities before the trend arrives and ride the trend all the way to the top.

About the Author

Melvin Peterson is an International consultant and educator on business and finance development. He has traveled over 22 countries and educated people on business and finance operations for many years. He has served in the military over 9 years and did a combat tour of duty in Iraq. He has several businesses and investment companies that have clients around the world. Melvin Peterson and David Anderson host and produce a syndicated Radio Talk Show called **Blackanomics** on XM satellite radio. This show broadcasts live on **channel 169 the Power** every weekend at 6:00 am EST. Melvin educate listeners on what is going on in the financial and business sector and empowers listeners to take control of their finances and generate multiple streams of income. This show educates listeners on business and financial strategies and gives solutions for entrepreneurs. Melvin Peterson is an Active Real Estate Agent in the state of Georgia and educates investors and clients in the opportunities in Real Estate and commercial properties. Melvin continues to serve by educating people on finances and business development for aspiring entrepreneurs and business leaders around the world

"I NEED A BIGGER WALLET"

LEETO PAYTON

BOOK NAME.

Dr. THOMAS MENSAH

CREATE A CONTACT BOARD AND
IDENTIFY EACH BUSINESS AND HOW
THEY CAN potentially HELP BUILD YOUR
BRAND.

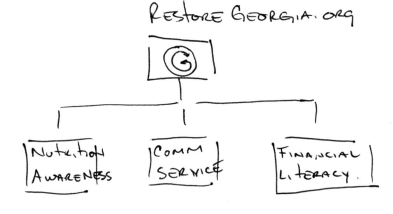

RESTORE GEORGIA.ORG

CREATE AN AUTORESPONDER FOR YOUR
NEW LEADS. THERE SHOULD BE A BUSINESS
PRESENTATION.

Made in the USA
Charleston, SC
20 May 2011